# The Ultimate Guide to Starting a Successful Lawn Mowing Business

Chapter 1: Understanding the Lawn Mowing Industry
   Overview of the lawn mowing industry.
   Market analysis and identifying target customers.
   Trends and opportunities in the industry.

Chapter 2: Developing a Business Plan
   Importance of a business plan for your lawn mowing venture.
   Key elements to include in your business plan.
   Financial considerations and projections.

Chapter 3: Legal and Licensing Requirements
   Understanding the legal and licensing obligations for a lawn mowing business.
   Registering your business and obtaining necessary permits.
   Insurance requirements and liability considerations.

Chapter 4: Acquiring the Right Equipment
   Essential equipment needed for a lawn mowing business.
   Evaluating and purchasing lawn mowers, trimmers, and other tools.
   Maintenance and care of your equipment.

Chapter 5: Setting Up Operations
   Establishing a professional image and branding for your business.
   Creating a pricing structure and determining competitive rates.
   Developing efficient scheduling and routing strategies.

Chapter 6: Marketing and Advertising
   Crafting a marketing strategy to attract customers.
   Utilizing online platforms, social media, and local advertising.
   Building strong customer relationships and referrals.

Chapter 7: Providing Exceptional Customer Service
   Importance of excellent customer service in the lawn mowing industry.

Communicating effectively with customers and addressing their needs.
Handling customer complaints and ensuring satisfaction.

Chapter 8: Hiring and Managing Employees
Expanding your business and hiring employees.
Effective recruitment strategies and selecting the right team.
Training, managing, and motivating your employees.

Chapter 9: Expanding Your Services and Growing Your Business
Identifying additional services to offer beyond lawn mowing.
Upselling and cross-selling opportunities.
Strategies for business growth and expansion.

Chapter 10: Overcoming Challenges and Ensuring Long-Term Success
Common challenges in the lawn mowing business and how to overcome them.
Staying competitive in a dynamic market.
Planning for the future and adapting to industry changes.

Conclusion:
Recap the key lessons and takeaways from the book.

Welcome to "The Ultimate Guide to Starting a Successful Lawn Mowing Business"! Whether you have a passion for working outdoors, have an entrepreneurial spirit, or simply want to take control of your own destiny, this book is your comprehensive resource to help you establish and grow a thriving lawn mowing business.

In these pages, I will share with you my knowledge, insights, and practical tips gained from years of experience in the industry. I have walked the same path you are embarking on right now, and I understand the challenges and opportunities that come with starting and running a successful lawn mowing business.

This book is designed to be your trusted companion throughout your journey, providing you with a step-by-step guide to navigate every aspect of building your business from the ground up. Whether you are just starting out or looking to take your existing lawn mowing business to new heights, you will find valuable information, strategies, and advice to propel you towards success.

We will begin by delving into the fundamental aspects of the lawn mowing industry, equipping you with a solid understanding of the market, its trends, and the opportunities that lie ahead. From there, we will move on to developing a comprehensive business plan that will serve as your roadmap to success.

Legal and licensing requirements can sometimes seem daunting, but fear not! I will demystify these complexities, guiding you through the necessary steps to ensure compliance and protect your business. We will also explore the importance of acquiring the right equipment and setting up efficient operations to maximize productivity and customer satisfaction.

No business can thrive without a strong marketing strategy, so we will delve into the world of effective marketing and advertising techniques tailored specifically for the lawn mowing industry. I will help you craft a compelling brand image, connect with your target audience, and differentiate yourself from the competition.

But it doesn't stop there. Providing exceptional customer service is paramount to your success, and we will uncover the secrets to building lasting relationships with your clients. Additionally, we will discuss the process of expanding your services, growing your business, and overcoming common challenges that may arise along the way.

Throughout this book, I will share practical tips, real-life examples, and invaluable insights garnered from my own experiences and the experiences of successful lawn mowing entrepreneurs. It is my sincere hope that by the end of this journey, you will be equipped with the knowledge and confidence to launch, manage, and scale a profitable lawn mowing business.

So, whether you are a seasoned landscaper looking to venture into the world of lawn mowing or an aspiring entrepreneur with a green thumb, I invite you to join me on this exciting journey. Together, let's pave the way to your success in the thriving and fulfilling world of lawn mowing!

Best regards,

E.G.

## Chapter 1: Understanding the Lawn Mowing Industry

The lawn mowing industry is a thriving sector within the broader landscaping and outdoor services market. As homeowners, businesses, and institutions prioritize well-maintained lawns and landscapes, the demand for professional lawn mowing services continues to grow. This presents a significant opportunity for aspiring entrepreneurs to establish and grow their own successful lawn mowing businesses.

Market Analysis:
   To embark on a successful lawn mowing venture, it is crucial to understand the market dynamics and identify your target customers. Conducting a thorough market analysis will help you determine the size of the local market, assess competition, and identify potential areas of growth. Consider factors such as population demographics, income levels, property types, and geographical

factors that may impact demand for lawn care services in your target area.

Trends and Opportunities:

The lawn mowing industry is not immune to evolving trends and changing customer preferences. Staying up-to-date with the latest trends and identifying emerging opportunities is key to staying competitive. Some notable trends in the industry include the growing demand for eco-friendly and sustainable lawn care practices, the increasing popularity of organic lawn treatments, and the adoption of technology-driven solutions such as automated scheduling and online payment systems. By embracing these trends, you can position your business as innovative and in tune with the needs of modern customers.

Seasonality and Business Considerations:

One important aspect of the lawn mowing industry is understanding the seasonality of the business. In most regions, lawn mowing services experience a peak demand during the spring and summer months when grass grows rapidly. It is crucial to plan and allocate resources accordingly to ensure efficient operations and customer satisfaction during the busy season. Additionally, developing a strategic pricing structure, offering flexible service plans, and diversifying your services beyond mowing (e.g., edging, weed control, fertilization) can help create a steady stream of revenue throughout the year.

Industry Regulations:

As with any business, the lawn mowing industry is subject to certain regulations and licensing requirements. Familiarize yourself with local and state regulations pertaining to business registration, licensing, insurance, and compliance with environmental standards. Understanding and adhering to these regulations will help protect your business, ensure credibility with customers, and avoid potential legal issues in the future.

The lawn mowing industry offers tremendous opportunities for entrepreneurs who are passionate about outdoor services and are eager to build a successful business. By conducting thorough market research, staying abreast of industry trends, and understanding the seasonality and regulations of the business, you will be well-equipped to make informed decisions and position your lawn mowing business for long-term success.

In the following chapters of this book, we will delve deeper into the crucial aspects of starting and running a successful lawn mowing business. From developing a business plan to acquiring the right equipment, marketing your services, and providing exceptional customer service, we will guide you through each step of the journey. Let's dive in and pave the way to your success in the world of lawn mowing!

## Market analysis and identifying target customers.

A key component of launching a successful lawn mowing business is conducting a comprehensive market analysis and identifying your target customers. By understanding the local market dynamics and the needs of your potential clients, you can tailor your services and marketing efforts to effectively meet their demands. In this section, we will explore the essential steps involved in market analysis and guide you through the process of identifying your target customers.

Understanding the Local Market

To begin your market analysis, it is crucial to gain a deep understanding of the local market in which you plan to operate your lawn mowing business. Start by researching the demographic profile of the area, including factors such as population size, age distribution, income levels, and homeownership rates. This information will help you gauge the potential demand for lawn care services and identify segments of the population that are most likely to require your services.

Additionally, consider the geographical characteristics of your target area. Determine the size and types of properties prevalent in the region, such as residential homes, commercial properties, or institutional campuses. This knowledge will enable you to tailor your services and pricing to suit the specific needs of your target market.

Assessing the Competition
Analyzing the competitive landscape is a crucial aspect of market analysis. Identify existing lawn mowing businesses and other landscaping service providers operating in your area. Study their services, pricing structures, target markets, and unique selling propositions. Understanding your competitors' strengths and weaknesses will allow you to position your business effectively and identify opportunities to differentiate yourself in the market.
When assessing the competition, pay attention to factors such as the number of competitors, their market share, and the level of customer satisfaction in the industry. This information will help you identify gaps or underserved segments in the market that you can target with your services.


Identifying Your Target Customers
    Once you have gained a solid understanding of the local market and assessed the competition, it's time to define your target customers. This involves creating a detailed profile of the individuals or businesses most likely to seek your lawn mowing services.
Consider the following factors when identifying your target customers:
1. Residential Customers:
   Homeowners: Determine the specific neighborhoods or residential areas where homeowners value well-maintained lawns and are willing to invest in professional lawn care services.
   Demographic Factors: Consider factors such as age, income levels, and lifestyle preferences that may influence their decision to hire lawn mowing services.
   Property Size: Identify properties with larger lawns or landscapes that require regular maintenance and are more likely to hire professional help.
2. Commercial Customers:

Small Businesses: Target local small businesses, such as office complexes, retail centers, or restaurants, that prioritize a well-groomed exterior to attract customers.
Property Management Companies: Establish relationships with property management companies responsible for maintaining commercial properties, including apartment complexes, condominiums, and industrial parks.
3. Institutional Customers:
Schools and Educational Institutions: Reach out to schools, colleges, and universities that require regular lawn maintenance to create a clean and inviting environment for students, staff, and visitors.
Government and Municipal Contracts: Explore opportunities to secure contracts with local government bodies or municipalities responsible for maintaining public parks, recreational areas, or community spaces.

By defining your target customers, you can focus your marketing efforts and tailor your services to meet their specific needs. Develop messaging and promotional strategies that resonate with your target audience, showcasing how your lawn mowing services can add value and convenience to their lives or businesses.

Market Research Techniques

To gather more insights about your target customers and validate your market analysis, consider using the following market research techniques:
1. Surveys: Conduct surveys to collect information about customers' preferences, satisfaction levels with existing lawn care services, and their willingness to pay for professional lawn mowing.
2. Focus Groups: Organize focus groups to delve deeper into customers' pain points, expectations, and desired features in lawn mowing services. This qualitative research can provide valuable insights for refining your business offerings.

3. Online Research: Utilize online resources, including social media platforms, industry forums, and local community groups, to gather feedback and engage in discussions with potential customers. This will help you understand their needs and preferences more intimately.
4. Customer Interviews: Interview potential customers, either in person or over the phone, to gain a deeper understanding of their lawn care requirements and the challenges they face with their current service providers.

By combining these market research techniques, you will gain valuable insights into your target customers' needs, preferences, and pain points. This information will help you tailor your services, pricing, and marketing messages to attract and retain your target audience effectively.

Remember, market analysis and identifying target customers is an ongoing process. As your business grows, regularly reassess the market dynamics and adjust your strategies to stay aligned with evolving customer preferences. By understanding your target market and tailoring your services accordingly, you will be well-positioned to launch and grow a successful lawn mowing business.
In the upcoming chapters of this book, we will delve into other crucial aspects of starting and running a successful lawn mowing business, including developing a business plan, acquiring the right equipment, and implementing effective marketing strategies. Let's continue this journey together and pave the way to your success in the lawn mowing industry!

**Trends and opportunities in the industry.**

To launch a successful lawn mowing business, it is crucial to stay ahead of the curve and embrace the latest trends and opportunities in the industry. Understanding and capitalizing on these trends will not only set you apart from the competition but also position your business for long-term growth. In this section, we will explore some of the noteworthy trends and opportunities in the lawn mowing industry.

Eco-Friendly and Sustainable Practices:
1. One prominent trend in the industry is the increasing demand for eco-friendly and sustainable lawn care practices. With growing environmental awareness, customers are seeking services that minimize the use of harmful chemicals and promote sustainable landscape management. Consider incorporating organic lawn treatments, composting, and natural pest control methods into your service offerings to cater to this environmentally conscious market segment.

Water Conservation:
2. As water scarcity becomes a concern in many regions, water-efficient lawn care practices are gaining popularity. Offer services such as smart irrigation system installation, water-efficient lawn maintenance techniques, and drought-resistant landscaping options. Position your business as an advocate for water conservation, helping customers maintain beautiful lawns while minimizing water usage.

Technology-Driven Solutions:
3. Technology is transforming the lawn care industry, offering opportunities for increased efficiency and enhanced customer experience. Embrace technology-driven solutions such as automated scheduling and routing software, online booking platforms, and mobile apps for easy communication with customers. These tools can streamline your operations, improve customer satisfaction, and provide a competitive edge.

Customized Service Plans:
4. Customers value personalized service that caters to their unique needs. Offer customized service plans that allow customers to choose from a range of options based on their

preferences and budget. This can include different levels of lawn maintenance, add-on services like landscaping or weed control, and flexible scheduling options. Tailoring your services to meet individual customer requirements can attract a loyal customer base and generate repeat business.

Niche Markets:
5. Consider targeting specific niche markets within the lawn mowing industry. This can include catering to high-end residential properties, retirement communities, or specialized properties like golf courses or sports fields. Niche markets often have specific requirements and are willing to pay a premium for specialized services. By focusing on these segments, you can carve out a unique position in the market and differentiate yourself from general lawn care providers.

Collaborations and Partnerships:
6. Explore collaborations and partnerships with other professionals in related industries, such as landscapers, garden centers, or property maintenance companies. By forming strategic alliances, you can expand your service offerings, cross-promote each other's businesses, and tap into new customer bases. Collaborations can also provide opportunities for referrals, allowing you to reach a wider audience and increase your customer acquisition.

Green Spaces in Urban Areas:
7. With the rise of urbanization, there is a growing demand for well-maintained green spaces in cities and urban areas. Target commercial properties, residential complexes, and public spaces in urban environments to offer your lawn mowing services. This segment presents significant growth potential and opportunities for long-term contracts or partnerships with property management companies and municipalities.

Seasonal Services Beyond Mowing:
8. Diversify your services beyond lawn mowing to create a steady stream of revenue throughout the year. Offer seasonal services such as spring and fall cleanups, snow removal, or holiday decoration installations. By providing additional services during slower mowing seasons, you can maximize your earning potential and maintain a consistent cash flow.

By capitalizing on these trends and opportunities, you can position your lawn mowing business as innovative, environmentally friendly, and customer-centric. Stay abreast of industry developments, adopt.

# Chapter 2: Developing a Business Plan

**The Importance of a Business Plan for Your Lawn Mowing Venture**

Starting a lawn mowing business is an exciting endeavor, but it requires careful planning and organization to ensure long-term success. One of the most critical steps in this process is developing a comprehensive business plan. A well-crafted business plan serves as a roadmap for your venture, guiding you through each stage of your business's growth and providing a solid foundation for decision-making. In this section, we will explore the importance of a business plan and discuss key elements that should be included.

Clarifying Your Vision and Goals:
A business plan forces you to clearly articulate your vision and goals for your lawn mowing business. It helps you define your company's mission, values, and the specific objectives you aim to achieve. By setting clear goals, you provide yourself with a direction and focus, making it easier to make strategic decisions and stay on track as you navigate the challenges of starting and growing your business.

Assessing Market Viability:
A business plan requires you to conduct a thorough market analysis, evaluating the demand for lawn mowing services in your target area, identifying your target customers, and understanding your competition. This analysis will help you assess the viability of your business idea and identify opportunities for differentiation. By understanding the market dynamics, you can refine your services and develop a unique value proposition that will attract customers and drive business growth.

Financial Planning and Budgeting:
A business plan forces you to analyze the financial aspects of your lawn mowing venture. It helps you estimate the initial startup

costs, projected revenue, and operating expenses. By creating a detailed financial forecast, including profit and loss statements, cash flow projections, and balance sheets, you gain a clear understanding of the financial feasibility of your business. This information is vital for securing funding from investors or lenders and for making informed financial decisions as your business grows.

Operational Structure and Resource Planning:

Your business plan should outline the operational structure of your lawn mowing business. This includes defining your organizational hierarchy, outlining roles and responsibilities, and determining the resources required to run your operations efficiently. By planning your resources, such as equipment, vehicles, and labor, you can anticipate and manage potential bottlenecks, ensure smooth operations, and optimize your efficiency and productivity.

Marketing and Sales Strategies:

A business plan provides a platform to develop your marketing and sales strategies. It allows you to identify your target market, understand their needs and preferences, and outline how you will reach and attract customers. You can define your pricing strategy, promotional activities, and customer acquisition tactics. With a well-defined marketing and sales plan, you can effectively position your lawn mowing business in the market and develop a compelling brand identity that resonates with your target audience.

Risk Assessment and Mitigation:

Launching a lawn mowing business comes with inherent risks and challenges. A business plan prompts you to conduct a thorough risk assessment and develop strategies for mitigating potential risks. By identifying and addressing potential obstacles and challenges upfront, you can minimize their impact on your business's success. This includes anticipating competition, regulatory compliance, and external factors such as weather conditions that may affect your operations.

Monitoring and Evaluation:
	A business plan is not a static document but rather a living tool that evolves with your business. It serves as a benchmark against which you can measure your progress and success. Regularly review and update your business plan to reflect changes in the market, industry trends, and your business's performance. By monitoring key metrics and evaluating your progress against the goals outlined in your plan, you can identify areas for improvement.

**Key Elements to Include in Your Business Plan**

	A well-structured and comprehensive business plan is essential for starting and growing a successful lawn mowing business. It serves as a roadmap, guiding your actions and decisions, and provides a clear understanding of your business's mission, goals, and strategies. In this section, we will discuss the key elements that should be included in your business plan.
Executive Summary:
1. The executive summary is a concise overview of your entire business plan. It should provide a compelling introduction to your business, highlighting its unique selling proposition, target market, and anticipated growth. While it appears at the beginning of your plan, it is often written last, as it summarizes the main points from the other sections.

Company Description:
2. The company description provides detailed information about your lawn mowing business. It should include your business name, legal structure, ownership details, and a brief history. Describe the services you will offer, your target market, and the competitive advantage that sets you apart from existing providers. Also, outline your vision and mission statements, highlighting your long-term goals and values.

Market Analysis:
3. The market analysis section examines the lawn mowing industry, your target market, and your competitors. Conduct a thorough analysis of the industry's size, growth potential, and trends. Identify your target customers, their demographics, and

their needs. Assess the competition, their strengths and weaknesses, and identify opportunities for differentiation and market positioning.

Organizational Structure and Management:

4. Provide an overview of your business's organizational structure and management team. Outline key roles and responsibilities, including the owner or founders, managers, and any other important personnel. Include their qualifications, experience, and contributions to the business. This section demonstrates your business's leadership and ensures that you have the right team in place to drive success.

Products and Services:

5. Describe in detail the lawn mowing services you will offer. Explain the scope of services, such as grass cutting, edging, trimming, and cleanup. Highlight any additional services, such as landscaping, fertilization, or pest control, that you may offer. Discuss how your services will meet the needs of your target customers and differentiate you from competitors.

Marketing and Sales Strategy:

6. In this section, outline your marketing and sales strategies to attract and retain customers. Identify your target market segments and outline how you will reach them through various channels, such as online marketing, local advertising, or direct mail. Detail your pricing strategy, including the rates for different services, and explain any promotional activities or special offers you plan to implement.

Financial Projections:

7. Provide detailed financial projections for your lawn mowing business. Include a startup budget, which outlines the initial costs required to launch your business, such as equipment purchases, vehicle expenses, and marketing expenses. Create a sales forecast, projecting revenue based on anticipated sales volume and pricing. Develop a cash flow

statement and income statement, reflecting your expected revenue and expenses over a specific period.

Operations and Management Plan:
8. Describe your day-to-day operations, including how you will schedule jobs, manage equipment, and ensure quality control. Discuss the systems and processes you will implement to streamline operations and maximize efficiency. Explain any technology or software you will utilize, such as scheduling software or customer relationship management tools.

Risk Assessment and Contingency Plan:
9. Address potential risks and challenges that your business may face and develop a contingency plan to mitigate these risks. Identify risks such as seasonal fluctuations, weather conditions, equipment breakdowns, or staffing issues. Describe how you will manage these risks and maintain continuity of operations.

Implementation Timeline:
10. Create a timeline that outlines the key milestones and activities required to launch and grow your lawn mowing business. Include important dates, such as obtaining necessary licenses and permits, purchasing equipment, hiring employees, and executing marketing campaigns. This timeline will serve as a guide for your progress and keep you on track as you work towards your business goals.

Appendix:
11. The appendix is an optional section where you can include additional supporting documents, such as market research data, competitor analysis, resumes of key team members, or lease agreements. It provides supplemental information for readers who may want to delve deeper into specific aspects of your business.

Remember, your business plan should be a dynamic document that evolves as your business grows and adapts to changing circumstances. Regularly review and update your plan to reflect new market trends, goals, and strategies. By including these key elements in your business plan, you will create a comprehensive roadmap that outlines your business's vision, strategies, and financial projections. This plan will not only guide your own actions but can also be presented to potential investors or lenders to secure funding and support for your lawn mowing business.

**Financial Considerations and Projections**

Launching and running a successful lawn mowing business requires careful financial planning and management. In this section, we will discuss key financial considerations and provide guidance on creating projections for your business.

Start-Up Costs:
Identify and estimate the initial costs required to start your lawn mowing business. This includes purchasing essential equipment such as lawn mowers, trimmers, blowers, and other tools. Consider vehicle costs if you need a truck or trailer to transport equipment. Don't forget to account for the costs of licenses and permits, insurance, marketing materials, and initial supplies. Be as detailed as possible when estimating your start-up expenses to ensure you have sufficient funds to get your business off the ground.

Revenue Projections:
Create a realistic sales forecast that outlines your expected revenue for the first few years of your business. Consider factors such as the number of clients you can realistically acquire, the average revenue per job, and the seasonal nature of the industry. Analyze market demand and competitive pricing to determine a competitive but profitable pricing structure for your services. Remember to account for seasonal

fluctuations in demand and adjust your projections accordingly.

Operating Expenses:
>    Identify and estimate your ongoing operating expenses. This includes costs such as fuel for equipment, maintenance and repairs, insurance premiums, marketing and advertising expenses, office supplies, and any other overhead costs specific to your business. Keep track of your expenses meticulously to maintain a clear understanding of your financial performance.

Cash Flow Management:
>    Maintaining positive cash flow is crucial for the sustainability of your lawn mowing business. Consider the timing of your expenses and revenue to ensure you have sufficient funds to cover your costs and maintain a healthy cash flow. Establish payment terms and policies with your clients to ensure timely payments and consider offering incentives for early payments. Implement effective invoicing and payment collection systems to streamline the process.

Profitability Analysis:
>    Regularly review and analyze your financial statements to assess the profitability of your business. Monitor your profit margin and compare it to industry benchmarks to ensure your pricing structure is sustainable. Identify areas where you can increase efficiency and reduce costs without compromising the quality of your services. Continuously seek opportunities to improve profitability through upselling, cross-selling, or expanding your service offerings.

Financing Options:
>    Consider the financing options available to support your lawn mowing business. This may include personal savings, loans

from financial institutions, or investments from partners or investors. Carefully evaluate the pros and cons of each option and choose the one that aligns with your financial goals and risk tolerance. Develop a repayment plan if you choose to seek external financing to ensure you can comfortably manage your debt obligations.

Remember, financial projections are estimates based on assumptions and market conditions. Regularly review and update your projections as you gather real data and insights from operating your business. This will allow you to make informed decisions and adapt your strategies to achieve long-term financial success.
By considering these financial aspects and creating accurate projections, you will have a clearer understanding of the financial feasibility of your lawn mowing business. This will enable you to make informed decisions, manage your resources effectively, and position your business for long-term profitability and growth.

## Chapter 3: Legal and Licensing Requirements

### Understanding the Legal and Licensing Obligations for a Lawn Mowing Business

When starting a lawn mowing business, it is crucial to understand the legal and licensing obligations that apply to your operation. Complying with these requirements not only ensures your business operates within the boundaries of the law but also instills trust and confidence in your clients. In this section, we will discuss the key legal and licensing considerations for your lawn mowing business.

Business Registration:

Before launching your lawn mowing business, you need to register it with the appropriate government authorities. Choose a legal structure for your business, such as a sole proprietorship, partnership, or limited liability company (LLC). Register your business name with the relevant agency and obtain any necessary permits or licenses required for operating a business in your jurisdiction. This step establishes your business as a legitimate entity and allows you to conduct business legally.

Insurance Coverage:
Obtaining proper insurance coverage is essential to protect your lawn mowing business from unforeseen events and potential liabilities. Consider securing general liability insurance, which covers damages to third parties or property while you are working on a client's premises. Additionally, explore commercial vehicle insurance if you use company vehicles for your business operations. Insurance coverage not only provides financial protection but also enhances your professional credibility.

Local Zoning and Ordinances:
Check local zoning regulations and ordinances to ensure you are compliant with any restrictions or requirements for operating a lawn mowing business in your area. Some neighborhoods or municipalities may have specific rules regarding noise restrictions, operating hours, signage, or equipment storage. Adhering to these regulations is essential to maintain a positive relationship with your community and avoid potential penalties or legal issues.

Licensing and Certification:
Research the licensing and certification requirements specific to the lawn care industry in your region. Depending on your location, you may need to obtain a landscaping or horticulture

license or certification to legally provide lawn mowing and related services. Some areas may require pesticide application certifications if you plan to offer pest control services. Familiarize yourself with the licensing process, including any exams or training requirements, and ensure you comply with all necessary regulations.

Employment and Labor Laws:
> If you plan to hire employees for your lawn mowing business, it is important to understand and comply with employment and labor laws. Familiarize yourself with regulations regarding minimum wage, overtime pay, employee classification (full-time, part-time, or independent contractor), and employee rights. Additionally, ensure you adhere to safety regulations, provide proper training, and maintain appropriate records related to your employees.

Contracts and Agreements:
> Developing clear and comprehensive contracts and agreements is crucial for protecting your business interests and maintaining transparent relationships with your clients. Create service agreements that outline the scope of work, pricing, payment terms, and any additional terms and conditions. Consider consulting with a legal professional to ensure your contracts comply with local laws and adequately protect your business.

Taxation:
> Understand your tax obligations as a lawn mowing business owner. Consult with an accountant or tax professional to determine the appropriate tax structure for your business and ensure you comply with all tax requirements, including income tax, sales tax, and payroll taxes. Maintain accurate financial records and keep track of deductible expenses to optimize your tax filings.

Intellectual Property:

Consider protecting your business's intellectual property, such as your business name, logo, or unique branding elements. Consult with a trademark attorney to explore options for trademark registration to safeguard your brand identity and prevent others from using similar marks that may cause confusion in the marketplace.

Ongoing Compliance:
Once your lawn mowing business is up and running, ensure ongoing compliance with legal and licensing obligations. Stay informed about any regulatory changes or updates that may affect your business and make necessary adjustments to remain in compliance. Regularly review and update your contracts, licenses, and insurance coverage to align with your evolving business needs.

Understanding and fulfilling the legal and licensing obligations for your lawn mowing business is essential for establishing a strong foundation and ensuring long-term success. Take the time to research and comply with these obligations to operate your business with integrity, professionalism, and legal compliance. By doing so, you will build a reputable and trustworthy lawn mowing business that clients can rely on.

**Registering Your Business and Obtaining Necessary Permits**

Registering your lawn mowing business and obtaining the necessary permits is a crucial step in establishing a legal and legitimate operation. This process not only ensures compliance with local regulations but also instills trust and confidence in your clients. In this section, we will guide you through the process of registering your business and acquiring the necessary permits.

Choose a Business Structure:
Before registering your lawn mowing business, determine the appropriate legal structure for your operation. Common

options include sole proprietorship, partnership, limited liability company (LLC), or corporation. Each structure has different legal and tax implications, so it's important to research and choose the one that best suits your business goals and circumstances. Consult with a business attorney or tax professional for guidance in this decision.

Registering Your Business Name:
Select a unique and memorable name for your lawn mowing business. Conduct a thorough search to ensure that the name is not already in use by another company in your industry. Once you have chosen a name, register it with the appropriate government agency. In most cases, this involves filing a "Doing Business As" (DBA) or fictitious name statement with your local county clerk's office. This step allows you to operate your business under a name other than your personal name.

Employer Identification Number (EIN):
Obtain an Employer Identification Number (EIN) from the Internal Revenue Service (IRS). An EIN is a unique nine-digit number that identifies your business for tax purposes. It is necessary if you plan to hire employees, open a business bank account, or file certain tax returns. You can apply for an EIN online through the IRS website, and the process is free of charge.

Licenses and Permits:
Research and identify the specific licenses and permits required to legally operate a lawn mowing business in your area. The requirements may vary depending on your location and the services you offer. Common licenses and permits include a general business license, landscaping license, and possibly pesticide application or chemical handling licenses. Contact your local city or county government offices to obtain information on the specific permits required and the application process.

Home-Based Business Considerations:
> If you plan to run your lawn mowing business from your home, check local zoning regulations to ensure you are compliant. Some areas have restrictions on operating certain businesses from residential properties. Review any Home Occupation Permits or zoning variances that may be required to operate your business legally. Additionally, consider any neighborhood or homeowners' association rules that may apply.

Insurance and Bonds:
> Obtain the necessary insurance coverage to protect your business and clients. General liability insurance is essential to cover any damages or injuries that may occur while providing your services. It provides financial protection in case of accidents, property damage, or bodily injury claims. Depending on your location and client requirements, you may also need to secure a surety bond, which acts as a guarantee of your performance and compliance with local regulations.

Ongoing Compliance:
> Once your business is registered and permits are obtained, it's important to maintain ongoing compliance with local regulations and licensing requirements. Stay informed about any changes to licensing or permit rules and renew your licenses and permits on time to avoid penalties or disruptions in your business operations. Keep accurate records of your business registrations and permits for easy reference and compliance verification.

> Remember, the specific registration and permitting requirements for your lawn mowing business may vary depending on your location. It's essential to research and comply with the regulations specific to your area. Engage with local government agencies, industry associations, or business support organizations to ensure you have the most up-to-date information and guidance.

By registering your business and obtaining the necessary permits, you establish a legal and trustworthy foundation for your lawn mowing business. This not only protects you from potential legal issues but also demonstrates professionalism and reliability to your clients. Take the time to navigate the registration and permitting process diligently, and you'll be well on your way to starting a successful lawn mowing business.

**Insurance Requirements and Liability Considerations**

When starting a lawn mowing business, it is crucial to understand the insurance requirements and liability considerations to protect your business, employees, and clients. Accidents and unforeseen events can happen, and having the right insurance coverage in place can provide financial protection and peace of mind. In this section, we will discuss the insurance requirements and liability considerations for your lawn mowing business.

General Liability Insurance:
General liability insurance is a fundamental coverage for any lawn mowing business. It protects you from financial losses in the event of property damage, bodily injury, or personal injury claims made by third parties. For example, if a client's property is damaged by your equipment or if someone is injured while you are mowing their lawn, general liability insurance would cover the associated costs, including legal fees, medical expenses, and property repairs. This insurance is essential to safeguard your business from potential lawsuits and to demonstrate your professionalism and commitment to your clients' well-being.

Commercial Auto Insurance:
If you use vehicles for your lawn mowing business, whether it's a truck, van, or trailer, commercial auto insurance is necessary. Personal auto insurance policies typically do not cover accidents or damages that occur while using the vehicle for business purposes. Commercial auto insurance provides

coverage for accidents, property damage, and bodily injury that may occur while you or your employees are driving company vehicles. It's important to accurately disclose the intended business use of the vehicle when purchasing this insurance to ensure full coverage.

Workers' Compensation Insurance:
If you plan to hire employees for your lawn mowing business, workers' compensation insurance is typically required by law. Workers' compensation provides coverage for medical expenses and lost wages in the event of work-related injuries or illnesses. It helps protect your employees and your business from financial strain due to workplace accidents. Consult with your local government or insurance provider to understand the specific workers' compensation requirements in your jurisdiction.

Professional Liability Insurance:
Professional liability insurance, also known as errors and omissions insurance, is worth considering for lawn mowing businesses that provide additional services such as landscaping design or lawn treatment recommendations. This insurance protects you in case a client claims that your professional advice or service resulted in financial loss or damage. It can cover legal fees and potential settlements if a client sues you for negligence, errors, or omissions in your professional services. While not always required, professional liability insurance can provide an extra layer of protection and peace of mind.

Bonding:
Being bonded is another way to demonstrate credibility and trustworthiness to your clients. A surety bond acts as a guarantee that you will fulfill your contractual obligations and meet any legal or licensing requirements. It offers financial protection to clients in the event of non-performance,

incomplete work, or property damage caused by your business. Some clients, especially larger commercial or government contracts, may require you to be bonded as a condition of working with them.

Umbrella Insurance:
Consider obtaining an umbrella insurance policy to provide additional liability coverage beyond the limits of your primary insurance policies. An umbrella policy offers an extra layer of protection in case a claim exceeds the coverage limits of your general liability, commercial auto, or other primary policies. It provides broader coverage and higher liability limits, helping protect your assets and business in the event of a significant claim or lawsuit.

Risk Management and Safety Measures:
While insurance coverage is crucial, it's equally important to implement risk management and safety measures to prevent accidents and minimize liabilities. Establish clear safety protocols for your employees, provide proper training, and enforce the use of personal protective equipment

# Chapter 4: Acquiring the Right Equipment

## Essential Equipment Needed for a Lawn Mowing Business

In the world of lawn mowing, having the right equipment is crucial for a successful and efficient operation. In this chapter, we will explore the essential equipment required to start and run a thriving lawn mowing business. From mowers to trimmers and safety gear, we will discuss each item's importance and how it contributes to the overall success of your business.

The equipment is the centerpiece of any lawn mowing business. It is essential to invest in high-quality equipment that suits the needs of your clients and the size of the properties you plan to service. Consider the following options:

Walk-Behind Mowers:
Walk-behind mowers are versatile and ideal for small to medium-sized lawns. Choose between push mowers for smaller areas and self-propelled mowers for larger or sloped landscapes. Ensure that the mower offers adjustable cutting heights to accommodate various grass types and conditions.

Riding Mowers:
Riding mowers are perfect for larger lawns, saving you time and effort. They come in various configurations, including rear-engine, lawn tractors, and zero-turn mowers. Evaluate the terrain and size of the lawns you expect to service to determine the appropriate riding mower for your business.

Trimming and Edging Tools
While mowers take care of the main lawn areas, trimming and edging tools provide the finishing touches. These tools ensure clean lines and precise cuts along sidewalks, driveways, flowerbeds, and other landscape features. Consider the following equipment:

String Trimmers:
> String trimmers, also known as weed eaters or weed whackers, are indispensable for reaching areas that mowers cannot access. Choose a gas-powered or electric trimmer based on your preferences and the size of the lawns you plan to service.

Edgers:
> Edgers create clean and defined edges along walkways and driveways. They help maintain a professional and polished look for your clients' lawns. Opt for a manual edger or a powered edger, such as a gas-powered or electric edger, depending on your budget and workload.

Safety Gear and Miscellaneous Equipment

Personal Protective Equipment (PPE):
> Prioritize safety by equipping yourself and your employees with the necessary PPE. This includes safety glasses, ear protection, sturdy work gloves, and steel-toe boots. Don't forget sunscreen, hats, and insect repellent for outdoor work during different seasons.

Trailer or Truck:
> A reliable mode of transportation is crucial for hauling your equipment to job sites. Depending on the size of your operation, consider investing in a trailer or truck with adequate towing capacity and storage options for your mowers and other tools.

Fuel and Oil Storage:
> Ensure you have proper storage containers for fuel and oil to comply with safety regulations. Invest in approved containers that are leak-proof and labeled correctly to prevent accidents or spills.

> Equipping your lawn mowing business with the essential tools and equipment is a fundamental step towards building a successful enterprise. Invest in high-quality mowers, trimmers, and safety gear to provide efficient services and maintain a professional image. Remember to choose equipment that aligns with the specific needs of

your target market and the size of the lawns you plan to service. By prioritizing quality and safety, you lay the foundation for a thriving lawn mowing business.

## Evaluating and purchasing lawn mowers, trimmers, and other tools.

In the world of lawn care, having the right equipment is essential for running a successful business. When starting a lawn mowing venture or upgrading your existing tools, it's crucial to evaluate and purchase the right lawn mowers, trimmers, and other tools. This chapter will guide you through the process of evaluating and purchasing these key equipment pieces, ensuring that you make informed decisions to maximize efficiency and profitability.

Evaluating Lawn Mowers

Before purchasing a lawn mower, it's important to assess your business requirements. Consider factors such as the size of the lawns you will be servicing, the terrain, and the frequency of use. This evaluation will help determine the appropriate type and size of lawn mower for your operations.

Researching Different Types of Lawn Mowers:

There are various types of lawn mowers available, each catering to different needs. Research popular options like walk-behind mowers, riding mowers, and zero-turn mowers. Understand their features, advantages, and limitations to identify the best fit for your business.

Comparing Brands and Models:

Once you have narrowed down the type of lawn mower you need, compare different brands and models. Consider factors such as durability, reliability, ease of maintenance, and customer reviews. Look for reputable manufacturers known for producing high-quality, long-lasting equipment.

Testing and Demo Opportunities:

Whenever possible, take advantage of testing and demo opportunities. Visit local dealers or equipment rental companies to try out different lawn mowers. This hands-on experience will help you gauge the comfort, maneuverability, and performance of each model, aiding in your decision-making process.

Considering Budget and Long-Term Investment:
While it's important to consider your budget, prioritize quality and durability over solely focusing on price. Investing in a reliable, high-quality lawn mower may result in long-term cost savings by reducing repairs and replacements. Calculate the return on investment based on the expected lifespan and performance of the chosen model.

Identifying Trimming and Edging Needs:
Evaluate the trimming and edging requirements of your lawn mowing business. Consider the size and complexity of the properties you will be servicing. Determine if you need string trimmers, edgers, or a combination of both to achieve professional results.

Comparing Trimmer Types:
Similar to lawn mowers, trimmers come in various types, including gas-powered, electric, and battery-operated models. Research the pros and cons of each type, considering factors such as power, runtime, and maintenance requirements. Choose the trimmer that aligns with your business needs and preferences.

Assessing Additional Tools:
In addition to lawn mowers and trimmers, evaluate other tools and equipment necessary for your business, such as leaf blowers, hedge trimmers, and chainsaws. Consider the quality, reliability, and compatibility with your existing equipment. Opt for versatile tools that can serve multiple purposes, reducing the need for excessive specialized equipment.

Balancing Cost and Quality:
While cost is a consideration, prioritize the quality and reliability of your tools. Invest in reputable brands known for producing durable equipment that can withstand the demands of daily use. Remember, cheap tools may require frequent repairs or replacements, leading to increased downtime and additional expenses in the long run.

Evaluating and purchasing lawn mowers, trimmers, and other tools is a critical step in building a successful lawn mowing business. Take the time to assess your business needs, research different equipment options, and compare brands and models. Consider factors such as durability, reliability, and long-term investment to make informed decisions. By investing in high-quality equipment that suits your specific requirements, you set the foundation for a thriving and efficient operation.

**Maintenance and care of your equipment.**

Equipment maintenance is crucial for the smooth operation and longevity of your tools. Regular maintenance and care not only help prevent breakdowns and costly repairs but also ensure optimal performance, efficiency, and client satisfaction. In this section, we will explore essential tips and practices for maintaining and caring for your equipment.

Create a Maintenance Schedule:
Establish a regular maintenance schedule for each piece of equipment you own. Develop a system to keep track of routine tasks such as oil changes, air filter replacements, blade sharpening, and general inspections. Consistency is key to ensuring your equipment remains in top condition.

Cleaning and Storage:
Clean your equipment after each use to remove grass clippings, dirt, and debris. Pay attention to the blades, cutting decks, and engine components. Use a brush or compressed

air to clear any clogs or buildup. Properly store your equipment in a clean, dry, and secure location to protect it from weather elements and potential theft.

**Oil Changes and Fluid Checks:**
Regularly change the oil in your lawn mowers and other engines as recommended by the manufacturer. Clean oil helps lubricate the internal components, reducing friction and wear. Additionally, check and top up other fluids, such as fuel and coolant, to ensure optimal performance.

**Blade Maintenance:**
The blades of your lawn mowers and trimmers are critical for achieving clean cuts. Inspect the blades regularly for signs of wear, damage, or dullness. Sharpen or replace them as necessary to maintain precision cutting. Dull blades not only produce uneven cuts but also put additional strain on the engine, resulting in decreased efficiency.

**Air Filters and Spark Plugs:**
Clean or replace the air filters regularly to prevent debris from clogging the engine. A clean air filter ensures proper airflow and combustion. Similarly, inspect and replace spark plugs when necessary to maintain reliable ignition and fuel efficiency.

**Belt and Drive System Checks:**
For equipment with belts or drive systems, regularly inspect them for signs of wear or tension issues. Loose or worn belts can lead to slippage, reduced performance, and even damage to other components. Adjust or replace belts as needed to maintain optimal operation.

**Professional Servicing:**
While regular maintenance is essential, consider professional servicing for your equipment at least once a year. Trained

technicians can identify potential issues, fine-tune settings, and conduct thorough inspections to ensure your tools are in peak condition.

Safety Precautions:
During maintenance, always prioritize safety. Disconnect spark plugs, remove batteries, or take other necessary precautions to prevent accidental starting. Wear appropriate protective gear, such as gloves and eye protection, when handling sharp blades or performing maintenance tasks.

Maintaining and caring for your equipment is a fundamental aspect of running a successful lawn mowing business. By establishing a regular maintenance schedule, cleaning and storing your equipment properly, and performing routine checks and tasks, you can maximize the lifespan and performance of your tools. Remember, well-maintained equipment not only saves you money on repairs but also enhances your professional image and client satisfaction.

# Chapter 5: Setting Up Operations

**Establishing a professional image and branding for your business.**

In the competitive world of lawn care, establishing a professional image and strong branding is vital to differentiate your business and attract customers. A professional image instills confidence, trust, and credibility among clients, while effective branding helps create recognition and loyalty. In this section, we will explore strategies to establish a professional image and develop a strong brand identity for your lawn care business.

Define Your Brand Identity:
Start by defining your brand identity—the values, personality, and characteristics that set your business apart. Consider your target market, your unique selling points, and the image you want to portray. This foundation will guide your branding efforts and shape your overall business image.

Logo and Visual Identity:
Create a visually appealing and memorable logo that represents your business. It should be simple, versatile, and reflect your brand identity. Consider hiring a professional designer who can translate your vision into a compelling logo. Extend your visual identity to other elements, such as color schemes, typography, and overall design aesthetic.

Professional Website:
In today's digital age, a professional website is essential for establishing credibility and providing information to potential customers. Ensure your website is visually appealing, user-friendly, and optimized for mobile devices. Include essential information like services offered, service areas, contact details, testimonials, and a

portfolio of your work. Regularly update your website with fresh content to showcase your expertise and stay relevant.

Uniforms and Dress Code:
Implement a dress code for yourself and your employees that aligns with your brand image. Well-maintained uniforms or consistent attire can enhance professionalism and create a cohesive team appearance. Consider adding your logo to uniforms, vehicles, and equipment to promote brand visibility.

Vehicle Branding:
Use your vehicles as moving advertisements by applying professional vehicle wraps or signage that display your logo, contact information, and key messages. This mobile branding creates brand awareness in the neighborhoods you service and enhances your professional image.

Consistent Brand Messaging:
Craft consistent and compelling brand messaging that aligns with your brand identity. Clearly communicate your unique value proposition, quality of service, and commitment to customer satisfaction. Use consistent language and tone in all your marketing materials, social media platforms, and customer interactions.

Online Presence and Social Media:
Leverage the power of social media platforms to build your brand and engage with your target audience. Create business profiles on platforms such as Facebook, Instagram, and LinkedIn. Regularly post relevant content, including before-and-after photos, landscaping tips, client testimonials, and updates about your business. Engage with your followers by responding to comments and inquiries promptly.

Professional Communication:
Maintain professionalism in all your communication channels. Answer phone calls and respond to emails promptly and courteously. Train your employees to deliver exceptional customer service,

ensuring that every interaction reflects your commitment to professionalism and customer satisfaction.

Establishing a professional image and strong branding for your lawn care business is key to attracting and retaining customers. Define your brand identity, create a visually appealing logo and website, implement a dress code, and leverage vehicle branding. Craft consistent brand messaging and maintain a strong online presence. By prioritizing professionalism and branding, you differentiate your business and build a strong foundation for success.

**Creating a pricing structure and determining competitive rates.**

Establishing a fair and competitive pricing structure is crucial for the financial success of your lawn mowing business. Determining the right rates requires careful consideration of various factors, including your costs, market conditions, and customer expectations. In this section, we will explore strategies for creating a pricing structure and determining competitive rates that balance profitability with client satisfaction.

Understand Your Costs:

Begin by understanding your costs to ensure your pricing covers all expenses and provides a reasonable profit margin. Consider both direct costs (e.g., fuel, equipment maintenance, insurance) and indirect costs (e.g., overhead expenses, marketing, administrative tasks). Calculate your total costs and determine how much revenue you need to generate to cover these expenses and achieve your desired profit margin.

Understanding your costs is essential for running a successful lawn care business. By comprehensively assessing your expenses, you can set appropriate pricing that covers your financial obligations while ensuring a reasonable profit margin. Start by identifying both direct and indirect costs. Direct costs include expenses directly related to providing your lawn care services, such as fuel, equipment maintenance, and supplies. Indirect costs encompass overhead expenses like insurance, marketing, administrative tasks, and equipment depreciation. Take the time to calculate and document these costs accurately to gain a clear understanding of your total expenses.

In addition to direct and indirect costs, it's crucial to consider other financial factors that may impact your business. These include any licensing or permit fees, taxes, and insurance premiums. It's also important to account for unforeseen expenses or emergencies by setting aside a contingency fund. Regularly reviewing and updating your cost analysis will help you stay informed about your financial standing and make informed decisions regarding pricing, budgeting, and overall profitability. Understanding your costs is the foundation for establishing a sustainable and profitable lawn care business.

Evaluate Market Conditions:

Research and analyze the local market to gain insight into pricing trends and competitors' rates. Consider factors such as the average rates in your area, the services offered by your competitors, and the quality of their work. While it's essential to be competitive, avoid setting your rates solely based on undercutting competitors. Instead, focus on providing value through high-quality service and professional standards.

Evaluating market conditions is a crucial step in establishing a successful lawn care business. By conducting thorough market research, you can gain valuable insights into your target audience, understand industry trends, and make informed decisions about your pricing, services, and marketing strategies. Start by researching your local market to determine the demand for lawn care services and identify potential competitors. Consider factors such as the number of existing lawn care businesses, their service offerings, pricing structures, and reputation. This information will help you gauge the level of competition and identify opportunities to differentiate your business.

Additionally, study the preferences and expectations of your target customers. Are they looking for basic lawn mowing services or do they also value additional services such as landscaping, pest control, or fertilization? Understanding their needs and desires will allow you to tailor your services and marketing messages accordingly. Stay up-to-date with industry trends and best practices, such as sustainable or eco-friendly lawn care practices, as these can give you a competitive edge. By thoroughly evaluating market conditions, you can position your lawn care business effectively, identify opportunities for growth, and develop strategies to stand out in the market.

Assess the Scope of Work:

Different properties have varying lawn care needs, which can impact the pricing structure. Evaluate factors such as the size of the lawn, complexity of landscaping features, frequency of service, and any additional services requested by the customer (e.g., edging, weed control, leaf removal). Develop a pricing structure that reflects these factors, allowing you to adjust rates based on the scope of work required.

Assessing the scope of work is a critical step in effectively pricing and planning for your lawn care business. Each property and client will have unique requirements, and it's essential to evaluate the specific tasks and services needed. Consider factors such as the size of the lawn, the complexity of landscaping features, and the frequency of service requested. Determine if additional services like edging, weed control, or leaf removal are necessary. By assessing the scope of work, you can accurately estimate the time, effort, and resources required for each job. This allows you to provide accurate quotes to customers and ensures that your pricing reflects the level of service and attention to detail you will provide. Understanding the scope of work helps you manage customer expectations and deliver exceptional results, leading to higher customer satisfaction and the potential for long-term client relationships.

Determine Pricing Models:

Consider different pricing models based on your business goals and customer preferences. Common pricing models in the lawn care industry include flat rates, hourly rates, and per-square-foot rates. Each model has its advantages and considerations, so choose the one that aligns with your business operations and client expectations.

Determining the right pricing model is a crucial aspect of running a successful lawn care business. There are several pricing models to consider, each with its own advantages and considerations. One common pricing model is the flat rate, where you charge a fixed fee for specific services. This approach offers simplicity and transparency for both you and your customers. Another option is an hourly rate, which is suitable for services that may vary in duration and complexity. Hourly rates provide flexibility and allow you to account for the time spent on each job accurately. Additionally, you may consider a per-square-foot rate, particularly for larger properties. This model takes into account the size of the lawn and ensures that your pricing is proportionate to the amount of work involved. Carefully consider your business goals, the average job duration, and the preferences of your target market to determine the pricing model that best suits your needs.

When selecting a pricing model, it's important to strike a balance between profitability and customer satisfaction. Avoid underpricing your services, as this can undermine your business's financial sustainability. However, setting prices too high can deter potential customers and make it challenging to compete in the market. It's also important to consider the perceived value of your services. If you offer additional services or unique expertise, you may be able to command a higher price. Additionally, take into account your costs, market rates, and the level of demand in your area. Regularly evaluate your pricing model and make adjustments as necessary to ensure it aligns with your business goals and remains competitive within the industry.

Factor in Profitability and Growth:

Setting competitive rates is not just about covering costs but also ensuring profitability and future growth. Account for your desired profit margin and consider your business growth plans. Pricing too low may attract customers initially, but it may not sustain long-term profitability. Strive for a balance between competitive rates and maintaining a healthy bottom line.

Factor in profitability and growth when determining the pricing for your lawn care business. While it's important to remain competitive, it is equally crucial to ensure that your pricing structure allows for a healthy profit margin. Consider your business expenses, including equipment maintenance, employee wages, insurance, and overhead costs. Calculate the revenue needed to cover these expenses and generate a reasonable profit. Additionally, factor in your growth plans and long-term financial goals. Pricing your services too low may attract customers initially, but it may not sustain profitability or support future business expansion. Strive for a balance that allows you to provide quality service, cover your costs, and achieve sustainable growth. Regularly monitor your financial performance, adjust pricing as needed, and focus on strategies that enhance both profitability and business expansion in the long run.

Value-Added Services:

Value-added services can be a valuable strategy to differentiate your lawn care business and attract customers. These additional services go beyond basic lawn maintenance and provide extra benefits and convenience to your clients. Consider offering services such as lawn aeration, fertilization, pest control, or landscaping consultations. These value-added services can enhance the overall health and appearance of the lawn, address specific customer needs, and showcase your expertise and versatility.

Lawn aeration, for example, involves perforating the soil to improve air circulation, water absorption, and nutrient uptake, leading to healthier grass. By providing this service, you can offer a comprehensive lawn care solution that sets you apart from competitors.

Fertilization is another value-added service that can significantly enhance the overall quality and appearance of the lawn. Offering tailored fertilization programs based on the specific needs of each lawn helps clients achieve lush, green, and thriving grass. Pest control services, such as controlling weeds or eliminating lawn-damaging insects, demonstrate your commitment to maintaining a healthy and pest-free environment for your clients' lawns.

Additionally, providing landscaping consultations can help clients with garden design, plant selection, and hardscape planning. This value-added service allows you to showcase your expertise and provide personalized recommendations to enhance the overall aesthetic appeal of their outdoor space.

When determining pricing for value-added services, consider the additional time, expertise, and materials required to deliver these services effectively. Communicate the benefits of these services to your clients, highlighting how they can improve the health, beauty, and functionality of their lawns. By offering value-added services, you not only increase your revenue potential but also strengthen customer satisfaction and loyalty, positioning your lawn care business as a comprehensive solution provider in the industry.

Pricing Adjustments and Seasonality:
Be prepared to adjust your pricing based on factors such as seasonal fluctuations, changes in supply costs, or shifts in demand. During peak seasons, when demand is high, you may consider implementing a premium pricing structure. Conversely, during slower periods, offering discounts or package deals can help attract new customers and maintain a consistent workload.

Pricing adjustments and seasonality play a significant role in the success of a lawn care business. Understanding how to adapt your pricing based on seasonal fluctuations and market conditions is essential for maintaining a consistent workload and maximizing profitability.

During peak seasons, such as spring and summer, when demand for lawn care services is high, you may consider implementing a premium pricing structure. Higher demand often means increased competition, and by adjusting your rates slightly higher, you can capture additional value for your services. However, be mindful of striking a balance between competitiveness and profitability to ensure that your pricing remains attractive to potential customers.

Conversely, during slower periods, such as winter or the off-season, it may be necessary to offer discounts or package deals to attract new customers and maintain a steady flow of work. By adjusting your rates strategically, you can encourage potential customers to choose your services over your competitors, even during less active periods.

It's crucial to keep an eye on market conditions, supply costs, and changes in demand throughout the year. Assess any fluctuations in fuel prices, equipment maintenance costs, or other overhead expenses that may impact your profitability. Regularly reviewing and adjusting your pricing based on these factors will help you stay competitive while ensuring your business remains financially sustainable.

Moreover, consider the specific needs and expectations of your customers during different seasons. For instance, in the autumn, there may be increased demand for services such as leaf removal or winterization. By offering seasonal services and adjusting your pricing accordingly, you can capitalize on these opportunities and generate additional revenue.

Communicate any pricing adjustments clearly to your customers, emphasizing the value they will receive despite the changes. Highlight the expertise, reliability, and quality of your services to justify any adjustments and demonstrate the ongoing commitment to customer satisfaction.

By understanding the seasonality of the lawn care industry and implementing appropriate pricing adjustments, you can optimize your business's revenue potential, maintain a consistent workload, and ensure the long-term success of your lawn care business.

Communicate Your Value:

When discussing pricing with potential customers, effectively communicate the value and benefits they will receive from your services. Emphasize your professionalism, reliability, quality of work, and any additional perks or guarantees you offer. Help customers understand that they are investing in a trusted partner who will take care of their lawn with expertise and care.


Creating a pricing structure and determining competitive rates for your lawn mowing business requires careful consideration of costs, market conditions, and customer expectations. Evaluate your costs, assess the scope of work, and research market rates. Choose a pricing model that aligns with your goals and factor in profitability and potential growth. By offering value, communicating your worth, and adjusting prices as needed, you can establish competitive rates that attract customers and ensure the financial success of your business.

### Developing efficient scheduling and routing strategies

Efficient scheduling and routing are essential components of running a successful lawn mowing business. Properly managing your schedule and optimizing your routes can help maximize productivity, reduce costs, and improve customer satisfaction. This chapter explores strategies and best practices for developing efficient scheduling and routing systems to streamline your operations and enhance your business's profitability.

Prioritize Geographic Proximity:
One of the key principles in efficient scheduling and routing is to prioritize jobs based on geographic proximity. Grouping together properties that are close to each other helps minimize travel time and fuel costs. By mapping out your service area and strategically planning your schedule, you can minimize unnecessary travel and increase the number of jobs completed in a day. Utilize mapping tools or specialized software to optimize routes and ensure efficient travel between locations.

Consider Property Characteristics:
When scheduling and routing, consider the unique characteristics of each property. Take into account factors such as lawn size, complexity, and specific client requests. Larger properties or those with intricate landscaping features may require more time to complete. By factoring in these considerations, you can allocate the appropriate amount of time for each job and avoid overbooking or rushing through tasks.

Account for Seasonal Demand:
Seasonal fluctuations can significantly impact the demand for lawn care services. Adjust your scheduling and routing strategies to accommodate these changes. For example, during the spring and summer months, when demand is high, consider extending your work hours or adding extra crews to meet customer needs. On the other hand, during the off-peak season, optimize your schedule by focusing

on routine maintenance tasks, equipment maintenance, or marketing efforts to attract new customers for the upcoming busy season.

**Efficient Crew Allocation:**

Efficient crew allocation is crucial for managing multiple jobs simultaneously. Assess the skills and strengths of your team members and assign tasks accordingly. Match experienced employees with complex or demanding jobs, while assigning simpler tasks to newer or less experienced team members. Effective crew allocation ensures that each job is completed efficiently and upholds your quality standards.

**Utilize Technology and Automation:**

Take advantage of technology and automation tools to streamline your scheduling and routing processes. Implement scheduling software that allows you to input job details, track progress, and allocate resources efficiently. Utilize GPS tracking systems to monitor crew locations and adjust routes in real-time. These technological advancements can save time, reduce errors, and enhance overall operational efficiency.

**Allow for Flexibility:**

While efficient scheduling and routing are essential, it's also important to allow for flexibility. Unforeseen circumstances such as weather conditions or equipment issues may require adjustments to your schedule. Maintain open lines of communication with your clients, so they understand that unforeseen circumstances can occasionally affect service timing. Having contingency plans and a responsive approach will help you handle unexpected changes while minimizing disruption to your operations.

Developing efficient scheduling and routing strategies is vital for maximizing the productivity and profitability of your lawn mowing business. By prioritizing geographic proximity, considering property characteristics, accounting for seasonal demand, allocating crews effectively, utilizing technology, and allowing for flexibility, you can streamline your operations, enhance customer satisfaction, and achieve sustainable growth. Implementing these strategies will position your business for success and establish a strong foundation for long-term profitability.

## Chapter 6: Marketing and Advertising

**Crafting a marketing strategy to attract customers.**

A well-crafted marketing strategy is essential for attracting and retaining customers for your lawn mowing business. In today's competitive market, it's crucial to effectively communicate your value proposition, build brand awareness, and differentiate yourself from competitors. This chapter explores key elements of a successful marketing strategy to help you attract new customers, retain existing ones, and position your lawn mowing business for long-term success.

Defining your target market is a crucial step in developing an effective marketing strategy for your lawn mowing business. To do this, consider the demographics, psychographics, and geographic location of your ideal customers. Demographics include factors such as age, gender, income, and household size. Psychographics delve into the interests, values, attitudes, and lifestyles of your target market. Understanding these aspects helps you tailor your messaging and services to resonate with their specific needs and desires. Geographic location is also important as it determines the areas you can effectively serve. By clearly defining your target market, you can focus your marketing efforts, allocate resources efficiently, and deliver tailored solutions that attract and retain the right customers for your lawn mowing business. Start by clearly defining your target market—the specific group of customers you aim to serve. Consider factors such as demographics, geographic location, and psychographics to understand their needs, preferences, and pain points. By understanding your target market, you can tailor your marketing messages, services, and pricing to appeal directly to their desires and effectively differentiate yourself from competitors.

Crafting a strong brand identity is crucial for establishing recognition and trust in the market. Develop a compelling brand name, logo, and tagline that accurately represent your business values, professionalism, and the quality of your services. Consistently apply your brand identity across all marketing materials, including your website, social media profiles, and printed collateral. This cohesive branding strategy helps you stand out, create a memorable impression, and build a strong brand image. Consistency is key, so ensure that your brand identity is applied across all touchpoints, from your website and social media profiles to your business cards and uniforms. Additionally, focus on communicating your unique value proposition and key differentiators, such as your attention to detail, personalized approach, or eco-friendly practices. By establishing a compelling brand identity, you can build trust, create recognition, and attract customers who resonate with your values and perceive your lawn mowing company as a reputable and trustworthy choice.

**Utilizing online platforms, social media, and local advertising.**

In today's digital age, utilizing online platforms, social media, and local advertising is essential for the success of your lawn mowing business. These channels provide a powerful means to reach and engage with your target audience, build brand awareness, and attract new customers. In this chapter, we will explore effective strategies and best practices for utilizing online platforms, leveraging social media, and implementing local advertising to maximize the visibility and growth of your lawn mowing business.

Start by establishing an effective online presence for your lawn mowing business. Create a professional website that showcases your services, highlights customer testimonials, and provides clear contact information. Optimize your website for search engines by incorporating relevant keywords, meta tags, and localized content to improve your ranking in search results. Additionally, claim and optimize your business profiles on online directories such as Google My Business, Yelp, and Bing Places. These platforms provide valuable visibility and enable potential customers to find and learn more about your lawn mowing services.

Social media platforms offer immense opportunities to connect with your target audience and promote your lawn mowing business. Create profiles on popular platforms such as Facebook, Instagram, Twitter, and LinkedIn, based on the preferences and demographics of your target market. Regularly post engaging content, such as lawn care tips, before-and-after photos, customer success stories, and seasonal promotions. Encourage customer interaction by responding to comments and messages promptly. Leverage social media advertising features to target specific demographics and geographic locations, boosting the visibility of your brand and services.

Local advertising plays a crucial role in attracting customers within your service area. Start by placing ads in local newspapers, community newsletters, or magazines that target homeowners or residents in your desired locations. Consider sponsoring community events, sports teams, or local charity initiatives to increase your visibility and demonstrate your commitment to the community. Direct mail campaigns, such as postcards or flyers, can also be effective in reaching potential customers. Ensure your advertising materials are visually appealing, highlight the benefits of your lawn mowing services, and include clear calls to action.

Online reviews and testimonials are powerful tools that can significantly influence potential customers' decision-making process. Encourage satisfied customers to leave reviews on platforms such as Google, Yelp, or your website. Display positive testimonials prominently on your website and social media profiles to showcase the quality of your services and build trust. Respond to reviews, both positive and negative, in a professional and courteous manner, showing your commitment to customer satisfaction.

Search engine optimization (SEO) techniques help improve your website's visibility in search engine results pages. Optimize your website by incorporating relevant keywords, creating informative and valuable content, and ensuring your website is user-friendly and mobile-responsive. Consider creating a blog where you can regularly publish articles related to lawn care, gardening tips, or seasonal maintenance guides. Collaborate with other local businesses or influencers in the home and garden industry to create guest posts or cross-promotions, increasing your online reach and visibility.

Join online communities and forums related to lawn care, gardening, or home improvement. Actively participate by answering questions, providing expert advice, and sharing valuable insights. This positions you as a knowledgeable and trusted authority in your field and helps to build brand awareness and credibility. Include a link to your website or social media profiles in your forum signature, allowing interested individuals to learn more about your lawn mowing services.

Utilizing online platforms, social media, and local advertising is essential for promoting and growing your lawn mowing business. Establishing a strong online presence, leveraging social media, implementing local advertising strategies, encouraging online reviews, implementing SEO techniques, and engaging with online communities can significantly boost your brand visibility, attract new customers, and ultimately contribute to the success of your lawn mowing business. Embrace these digital marketing strategies and harness the power of local advertising to stay ahead of the competition and build a strong customer base.

**Building strong customer relationships and referrals.**

Building strong customer relationships and generating referrals are key factors in the success of your lawn mowing business. Satisfied customers not only become loyal clients but also serve as valuable brand advocates, recommending your services to their friends, family, and neighbors. In this chapter, we will explore effective strategies and best practices for building strong customer relationships, exceeding customer expectations, and encouraging referrals to drive the growth of your lawn mowing business.

Providing exceptional customer service is the foundation of building strong customer relationships. Train your team to be friendly, professional, and attentive to customers' needs. Respond promptly to inquiries, be proactive in communicating scheduling changes, and address any concerns or issues promptly and effectively. By consistently exceeding customer expectations, you create a positive experience that fosters loyalty and encourages customers to recommend your services to others.

Take a personalized approach to your customer interactions. Get to know your customers on an individual basis and make an effort to understand their specific lawn care needs and preferences. Tailor your services accordingly and provide personalized recommendations or advice to help them achieve their desired lawn appearance. By showing genuine interest and offering customized solutions, you establish a strong rapport and build trust with your customers, increasing the likelihood of repeat business and referrals.

Maintaining regular communication with your customers is crucial for building lasting relationships. Send out regular newsletters or email updates with valuable lawn care tips, seasonal reminders, or exclusive promotions. Schedule follow-up calls or visits to ensure customer satisfaction and address any ongoing lawn care needs. By staying engaged and demonstrating your commitment to their lawn care, you reinforce the value of your services and nurture long-term relationships.

Rewarding customer loyalty is an effective way to strengthen relationships and encourage referrals. Implement a customer loyalty program that offers incentives for repeat business or referrals. This could include discounts on future services, referral bonuses, or exclusive access to special offers. Not only does this show appreciation for your customers' support, but it also motivates them to continue using your services and refer others, expanding your customer base.

Actively seek feedback from your customers to gauge their satisfaction and identify areas for improvement. This can be done through post-service surveys, online reviews, or direct feedback channels. Take feedback seriously and use it as an opportunity to refine your services and address any concerns. By actively seeking and acting upon customer feedback, you demonstrate your commitment to providing the best possible experience, which further strengthens customer relationships.

Word-of-mouth referrals are powerful endorsements for your lawn mowing business. Encourage satisfied customers to refer your services to their friends, family, and neighbors. Request referrals through personalized emails, thank-you cards, or loyalty program incentives. Consider implementing a referral program that rewards customers for successful referrals. Leverage positive online reviews and testimonials as social proof to reinforce your reputation and attract new customers.

Become an active member of your local community and engage with residents and organizations. Participate in community events, sponsor local sports teams or charitable initiatives, or offer free lawn care workshops or demonstrations. By establishing a presence and contributing positively to your community, you build brand visibility and reputation, which can lead to increased referrals and customer trust.

Building strong customer relationships and generating referrals are vital for the growth and success of your lawn mowing business. By delivering exceptional customer service, personalizing your approach, maintaining regular communication, implementing loyalty programs, seeking customer feedback, and fostering community engagement, you create a positive experience that turns satisfied customers into loyal brand advocates. Nurture these relationships, leverage customer referrals, and watch your lawn mowing business thrive.

## Chapter 7: Providing Exceptional Customer Service

**Importance of excellent customer service in the lawn mowing industry.**

Customer satisfaction is a crucial metric for any lawn mowing business. Satisfied customers are more likely to remain loyal, provide positive reviews and referrals, and continue using your services season after season. Excellent customer service directly contributes to customer satisfaction by addressing their needs, promptly resolving any issues or concerns, and consistently delivering on your promises. By making customer satisfaction a top priority, you ensure that your clients are happy with their lawn care experience. Enhancing customer satisfaction is a critical objective for your lawn care business. By providing a high level of service and exceeding customer expectations, you can ensure that your clients are not only satisfied but delighted with their experience. This can be achieved by promptly responding to inquiries and concerns, maintaining clear and open lines of communication, consistently delivering quality work, and paying attention to the specific needs and preferences of each customer. Additionally, seeking feedback and actively addressing any issues or areas for improvement demonstrates your commitment to customer satisfaction. By focusing on enhancing customer satisfaction, you foster loyalty, generate positive reviews and referrals, and establish a strong reputation in the lawn care industry.

**Communicating effectively with customers and addressing their needs.**

Effective communication is a fundamental element of running a successful lawn mowing business. It not only allows you to understand and address your customers' needs but also builds trust, fosters satisfaction, and establishes long-term relationships. In this chapter, we will explore strategies and best practices for communicating effectively with customers and ensuring their needs are met throughout their lawn care journey.

Clear and Timely Communication:
Clear and timely communication is the cornerstone of effective customer service. Respond promptly to customer inquiries, whether they come through phone calls, emails, or social media messages. Be proactive in providing updates on scheduling changes, service details, or any other relevant information. Clear communication ensures that customers are well-informed and reassured about their lawn care services, resulting in a positive experience.

Active Listening and Understanding Customer Needs:
Effective communication goes beyond simply relaying information; it involves active listening and understanding the unique needs of your customers. Take the time to listen attentively to their requests, concerns, and preferences. Ask probing questions to gain a deeper understanding of their expectations. By demonstrating genuine

interest and empathy, you can tailor your services to meet their specific requirements and deliver a personalized lawn care experience.

Provide Detailed Service Information. Customers appreciate transparency and comprehensive information about the services they are receiving. Clearly communicate the scope of your lawn mowing services, including the frequency of visits, the specific tasks performed, and any additional services available. Provide written service agreements or contracts that outline the terms and conditions, pricing, and any guarantees or warranties. By providing detailed service information, you set clear expectations and build trust with your customers.

Empowering your customers with knowledge and resources is an effective way to enhance communication and address their needs. Educate them about proper lawn care practices, seasonal maintenance tips, and proactive measures they can take to keep their lawns healthy. This can be done through blog posts, social media content, or informational newsletters. By sharing valuable insights and guidance, you position yourself as a trusted authority and build credibility with your customers.

Professional and Courteous Communication is key. Maintaining a professional and courteous demeanor in all customer interactions is essential. Whether it's speaking with customers in person, over the phone, or through written communication, always be respectful, attentive, and polite. Use clear and concise language, avoid technical jargon, and address any concerns or complaints promptly and professionally. Professional communication fosters trust, establishes a positive impression of your business, and promotes a positive customer experience.

Following up with customers after providing your lawn care services demonstrates your commitment to their satisfaction. Reach out to them to ensure that they are happy with the results and address any further questions or concerns they may have. Additionally, actively seek customer feedback through surveys, online reviews, or feedback forms. Use this feedback as an opportunity for improvement and to fine-tune your services to better meet customer needs. mowing industry.

**Handling customer complaints and ensuring satisfaction.**

Customer complaints are inevitable in any business, including the lawn mowing industry. How you handle these complaints can make a significant impact on customer satisfaction and the reputation of your business. In this chapter, we will discuss effective strategies for handling customer complaints and ensuring their satisfaction, ultimately turning potential negatives into opportunities for growth and improved customer relationships.

Create a Culture of Listening. One of the most crucial aspects of handling customer complaints is creating a culture of listening within your lawn mowing business. Train your staff to actively listen to customers' concerns, allowing them to express their frustrations or dissatisfaction freely. Provide a safe and nonjudgmental environment where customers feel heard and valued. By fostering a culture of listening, you demonstrate your commitment to understanding and addressing customer needs.

When a customer complaint arises, it is essential to respond promptly and empathetically. Acknowledge their concerns and express genuine empathy for any inconvenience or dissatisfaction they may have experienced. Responding promptly shows that you value their feedback and are committed to resolving the issue swiftly. By addressing complaints with empathy, you can help defuse tension and build trust with the customer.

Always investigate and Understand the Issue. To effectively address customer complaints, take the time to investigate and understand the root cause of the problem. Gather all relevant information from the customer, your staff, or any other involved parties. Thoroughly assess the situation and avoid making assumptions. This diligent approach allows you to address the issue comprehensively and prevent similar problems from occurring in the future. When appropriate, offer a sincere apology to the customer. Taking responsibility for any mistakes or shortcomings demonstrates accountability and a commitment to resolving the issue. Avoid making excuses or shifting blame, as this can further escalate the situation. Instead, focus on finding a solution and assuring the customer that their concerns are being taken seriously.

After understanding the customer's complaint, provide an appropriate solution or compensation to resolve the issue. This could involve redoing the service, offering a discount or refund, or providing additional services at no cost. Tailor your response to the specific situation and the customer's preferences. By offering a fair and satisfactory resolution, you show your commitment to customer satisfaction and the willingness to make things right. Ensure clear and transparent communication regarding the resolution of the complaint. Explain the steps taken to address the issue and outline any actions you will be taking to prevent a recurrence. Clearly communicate any changes or improvements you will implement to prevent similar problems in the future. By being transparent and proactive, you instill confidence in the customer that their feedback has been taken seriously.

Following the resolution of a complaint, make it a priority to follow up with the customer. Reach out to ensure their satisfaction and inquire if there is anything else you can do to improve their experience. This gesture shows that you genuinely care about their satisfaction and allows you to further strengthen the customer relationship. Additionally, encourage customers to provide feedback on their overall experience, both positive and negative. This feedback can help you identify trends or areas for improvement and implement necessary changes. Every customer complaint should be seen as an opportunity for learning and improvement. Regularly review and analyze customer complaints to identify any recurring issues or patterns. Use this information to implement process improvements, refine training protocols, or make necessary adjustments to avoid similar complaints in the future. By continuously learning from customer feedback, you demonstrate your commitment to providing excellent service and enhancing customer satisfaction.

Handling customer complaints effectively is vital for ensuring customer satisfaction and the success of your lawn mowing business. By creating a culture of listening, responding promptly and empathetically, investigating and understanding the issue, apologizing and taking responsibility, providing a fair solution, communicating clearly, following up, and continuously learning from feedback, you can turn customer complaints into opportunities for improvement and building stronger customer relationships.

## Chapter 8: Hiring and Managing Employees

**Expanding your business and hiring employees.**

As your lawn care business grows, there will come a point when expanding and hiring employees becomes necessary. This expansion opens up new opportunities for increased revenue, expanded service offerings, and improved customer satisfaction. However, it also presents unique challenges and considerations. In this chapter, we will explore the key aspects of expanding your business and hiring employees, providing you with valuable insights and practical tips to ensure a successful transition and continued growth.

Assessing Business Readiness for Expansion: Before embarking on the expansion journey, it's crucial to assess the readiness of your lawn care business. Evaluate your current workload, customer base, and financial stability. Ensure that your business processes, systems, and infrastructure can handle additional work and employee management. Conduct a thorough analysis of the market demand and competition in your area to gauge the potential for growth. By conducting a comprehensive assessment, you can make informed decisions about when and how to expand.

To effectively expand your business, you need a well-defined growth strategy. Determine your expansion goals and objectives, whether it's increasing the number of clients, expanding service offerings, or entering new markets. Develop a detailed plan outlining the steps, timelines, and resources required to achieve these goals. Consider factors such as marketing and advertising, operational capacity, equipment investment, and financial projections. A solid growth strategy will serve as a roadmap for your expansion and help you stay focused and organized.

Expanding your business often means hiring a team of employees to assist with the increased workload. Hiring the right team members is crucial for maintaining service quality and customer satisfaction. Clearly define the roles and responsibilities you need to fill and create detailed job descriptions. Seek out qualified candidates through various recruitment channels, such as online job boards, local advertisements, or referrals. Conduct thorough interviews and background checks to ensure you select the best fit for your business. Once you have hired employees, provide them with proper training, clear expectations, and ongoing support to set them up for success.

As you bring employees on board, effective performance management becomes essential. Establish clear performance expectations and provide regular feedback and coaching. Implement a performance evaluation system to assess employee performance and identify areas for improvement. Offer opportunities for professional development and growth to motivate and retain your team members. By effectively managing employee performance, you create a productive and engaged workforce that contributes to the success of your expanding business. Building a Strong Company Culture as your team grows, it's important to foster a strong company culture that aligns with your business values and goals. Clearly communicate your vision, mission, and core values to your employees. Create a positive and inclusive work environment that promotes teamwork, respect, and open communication. Celebrate achievements, recognize employee contributions, and promote a sense of belonging and camaraderie. A strong company culture helps to attract and retain top talent and cultivates a positive reputation for your business.

Expanding your business and hiring employees also means navigating legal requirements and compliance. Familiarize yourself with labor laws, tax obligations, and insurance requirements specific to your region or country. Consult with legal and financial professionals to ensure you meet all legal obligations and have the necessary documentation and contracts in place. Compliance not only protects your business but also instills confidence in your employees and clients.

Scaling Operations and Infrastructure: As your business expands, it's important to scale your operations and infrastructure accordingly. Invest in the necessary equipment, tools, and technology to meet the increased demand efficiently. Streamline your processes and workflows to ensure smooth operations and minimize bottlenecks. Implement systems for scheduling, invoicing, and customer management to support your growing customer base. Continuously evaluate and adjust your operational strategies to optimize efficiency and maintain service quality.

Marketing and Business Development: Expanding your business requires an effective marketing and business development strategy to attract new clients and increase brand awareness. Review and adjust your marketing initiatives to align with your growth goals. Leverage digital marketing channels, such as social media, online advertising, and search engine optimization, to reach a broader audience. Network with local businesses, participate in community events, and seek referrals from satisfied customers. A robust marketing and business development plan will help fuel your expansion efforts and generate a steady stream of new clients.

Expanding your lawn care business and hiring employees is an exciting phase that brings new opportunities for growth and success. By assessing your readiness, developing a growth strategy, hiring and managing a capable team, building a strong company culture, ensuring legal compliance, scaling operations and infrastructure, and implementing effective marketing and business development strategies, you can navigate this expansion phase with confidence and achieve sustainable growth for your business.

## Effective recruitment strategies and selecting the right team

Building a successful lawn care business requires a dedicated and skilled team. Effective recruitment strategies and selecting the right individuals are crucial steps in creating a high-performing workforce. In this chapter, we will explore various recruitment techniques and provide insights into selecting the right team members for your lawn care business. By implementing effective recruitment strategies and making informed hiring decisions, you can build a team that contributes to the success and growth of your business.

Clearly Define Job Roles and Requirements: Before starting the recruitment process, it's essential to clearly define the job roles and requirements for your lawn care business. Identify the specific tasks, responsibilities, and skills needed for each position. Consider the qualifications, experience, and certifications required for different roles, such as lawn mowing specialists, landscapers, or irrigation technicians. By clearly outlining the job expectations, you attract candidates who possess the necessary skills and qualifications.

A targeted recruitment plan helps you reach qualified candidates efficiently. Utilize a combination of online and offline recruitment channels to broaden your candidate pool. Online platforms such as job boards, social media, and your business website are effective for reaching a wider audience. Additionally, consider local advertising, community job fairs, and industry-specific publications to target potential candidates in your area. Tailor your recruitment plan to the specific positions you are hiring for, ensuring that you reach individuals with the desired skill set and experience.

A thorough screening and interview process are crucial for identifying the most qualified candidates. Review resumes, applications, and cover letters to shortlist candidates who meet the required qualifications. Conduct initial phone or video interviews to assess candidates' communication skills and basic knowledge. Invite promising candidates for in-person or virtual interviews where you can delve deeper into their experience, problem-solving abilities, and cultural fit. Use behavioral and situational questions to gauge their skills and how they handle specific work scenarios. Finding team members who align with your company culture and values is as important as evaluating their technical skills. During the interview process, assess whether candidates share similar values, work ethics, and attitudes towards customer service and teamwork. Consider the importance of punctuality, attention to detail, and a strong work ethic in your lawn care business. Look for individuals who demonstrate a passion for the industry and a commitment to providing exceptional service to your clients.

In addition to interviews, consider conducting skills assessments and practical tests to evaluate candidates' abilities. For example, you can have candidates demonstrate their lawn mowing or landscaping skills by performing a practical task or providing samples of their previous work. This hands-on evaluation allows you to assess their proficiency, attention to detail, and ability to meet quality standards. To ensure the reliability and professionalism of potential hires, it's crucial to check references and conduct background checks. Contact the references provided by candidates to gain insights into their past work performance, reliability, and interpersonal skills. Additionally, consider conducting background checks to verify employment history, qualifications, and any relevant certifications. These checks provide reassurance that you are making informed hiring decisions and safeguarding your business reputation.

Attracting and retaining top talent in the lawn care industry often requires offering competitive compensation and benefits. Research industry standards and local market rates to ensure you provide a fair and competitive salary package. Consider additional benefits such as healthcare coverage, retirement plans, paid time off, or performance incentives to incentivize your employees and demonstrate your commitment to their well-being. Once you have selected the right team members, invest in their ongoing training and development. Provide comprehensive onboarding to familiarize new hires with your business processes, safety procedures, and quality standards. Offer continuous training opportunities to enhance their skills and keep them up to date with industry advancements. By investing in the growth and development of your team, you create a motivated and skilled workforce that can deliver

Effective recruitment strategies and selecting the right team members are critical for the success of your lawn care business. By clearly defining job roles and requirements, developing a targeted recruitment plan, implementing a thorough screening process, assessing cultural fit, conducting skills assessments, checking references, offering competitive compensation and benefits, and providing ongoing training and development, you can assemble a high-performing team that aligns with your business goals and values. A well-selected team will contribute to the growth, reputation, and success of your lawn care business in the long run.

**Training, managing, and motivating your employees**

In the lawn care business, your employees are the backbone of your operations. Properly training, managing, and motivating your team members is essential for maintaining service quality, efficiency, and overall business success. In this chapter, we will explore the key aspects of training, managing, and motivating employees in the lawn care industry. By implementing effective strategies and creating a positive work environment, you can foster employee growth, job satisfaction, and long-term loyalty.

Effective employee training starts with a comprehensive onboarding process. Introduce new hires to your company culture, values, and expectations. Provide them with an overview of your business operations, safety protocols, and customer service standards. Assign experienced team members as mentors to guide new employees and ensure a smooth transition. Develop a training program that covers technical skills, equipment operation, landscaping techniques, and customer interaction. Regularly assess employee knowledge and provide ongoing training opportunities to keep skills sharp and up-to-date.

Strong communication is vital for managing and motivating employees. Clearly communicate job responsibilities, performance expectations, and key performance indicators (KPIs). Foster an open-door policy where employees can freely express their ideas, concerns, and suggestions. Regularly hold team meetings to discuss goals, provide feedback, and address any challenges. Encourage two-way communication to build trust and strengthen the team dynamic. Effectively managing employee performance involves setting clear goals and providing regular feedback. Establish performance metrics and targets that align with your business objectives. Conduct periodic performance evaluations to assess employee progress and identify areas for improvement. Provide constructive feedback, highlighting both strengths and areas that require development. Recognize and reward outstanding performance to motivate and inspire your team members. Offering opportunities for advancement and career growth can also boost employee morale and engagement.

Empowering your employees and granting them autonomy can lead to increased job satisfaction and productivity. Delegate responsibilities and allow team members to make decisions within their roles. Encourage innovative thinking and problem-solving. When employees feel trusted and valued, they are more likely to take ownership of their work and contribute to the success of your business.

Promote a positive work environment that fosters teamwork and collaboration. Organize team-building activities to improve camaraderie and morale. Encourage collaboration between team members on projects, sharing best practices, and learning from each other's experiences. Foster a culture of mutual support and respect, where employees feel comfortable seeking help and offering assistance to their colleagues. Recognizing and rewarding your employees' efforts is crucial for maintaining motivation and job satisfaction. Implement a recognition program to acknowledge outstanding performance, such as employee of the month awards or performance-based incentives. Offer competitive compensation and benefits packages to attract and retain top talent. Celebrate milestones, achievements, and team successes to reinforce a positive work environment and encourage a sense of pride in their work.

Invest in the continued training and professional development of your employees. Offer opportunities for skill enhancement through workshops, seminars, industry conferences, or online courses. Encourage certifications or professional memberships that demonstrate their expertise and dedication. By investing in your employees' growth, you not only enhance their abilities but also show that you value their long-term career development.

Promoting employee wellness and work-life balance is crucial for maintaining a motivated and productive workforce. Provide a safe and healthy work environment, offer flexibility when possible, and promote work-life balance through fair scheduling practices. Encourage employees to take breaks and prioritize self-care. Consider wellness initiatives such as employee assistance programs, wellness challenges, or gym memberships to support their overall well-being.

Training, managing, and motivating your employees are integral parts of running a successful lawn care business. By implementing comprehensive onboarding and training programs, establishing clear communication and expectations, providing regular feedback, empowering your team, fostering collaboration, recognizing and rewarding their efforts, investing in their professional development, and promoting employee wellness, you can create a motivated and dedicated workforce that contributes to the growth and success of your business. Remember, happy and engaged employees lead to satisfied customers and long-term business prosperity.

## Chapter 9: Expanding Your Services and Growing Your Business

**Identifying additional services to offer beyond lawn mowing.**

Expanding the range of services offered by your lawn care business can provide new revenue streams, attract a wider customer base, and increase customer satisfaction. While lawn mowing is a fundamental service, offering additional services allows you to cater to a broader range of customer needs and differentiate yourself from competitors. In this chapter, we will explore the importance of identifying and incorporating additional services into your lawn care business. By assessing market demands, understanding customer preferences, and leveraging your existing expertise, you can successfully expand your service offerings and drive business growth.

To identify additional services that align with your lawn care business, it is crucial to conduct thorough market research. Analyze your target market to understand their needs, preferences, and pain points. Consider surveying existing customers to gather feedback and insights on the services they desire. Explore industry trends and competitor offerings to identify gaps in the market that your business can fill. By conducting comprehensive market research, you can gain valuable information to guide your decision-making process. Consider your team's skills, expertise, and available resources when determining additional services to offer. Evaluate the capabilities of your workforce and identify areas where they can expand their skill set or obtain necessary certifications. Leverage your existing equipment and infrastructure to provide new services more efficiently. For example, if your team already has experience with lawn maintenance, offering services like fertilization, weed control, or irrigation system installation can be a natural extension. By building on your existing strengths, you can expand your service offerings while maintaining quality and efficiency.

Look beyond traditional lawn care services and consider diversifying your offerings to meet a broader range of customer needs. Some potential additional services to consider include:

> Landscape Design and Installation: Offer comprehensive landscape design and installation services to transform outdoor spaces into beautiful and functional environments. This can include plant selection, hardscaping, and landscape lighting.
>
> Tree and Shrub Care: Expand your services to include tree and shrub pruning, trimming, and removal. Provide expert advice on tree health and offer solutions for pest control and disease management.
>
> Seasonal Cleanup and Maintenance: Offer seasonal cleanup services to prepare lawns and landscapes for different

seasons. This can include leaf removal, mulching, and winterizing services.

Lawn Aeration and Overseeding: Provide lawn aeration and overseeding services to improve soil health, enhance grass growth, and promote a lush and healthy lawn.

Pest Control: Offer pest control services to address common lawn pests, such as grubs, mosquitoes, and ticks. Provide solutions for pest prevention and treatment.

When identifying additional services, it's crucial to evaluate their profitability and demand. Assess the potential revenue and profit margins of each service offering, considering factors such as labor costs, equipment requirements, and market demand. Conduct a cost-benefit analysis to ensure that the additional services align with your business goals and contribute to your overall profitability. Focus on services that are in high demand, have the potential for recurring revenue, and can be efficiently integrated into your existing operations.

Once you have identified the additional services to offer, develop a marketing strategy to promote them effectively. Update your website, social media profiles, and marketing materials to reflect the expanded service offerings. Highlight the benefits and value of these services to potential customers. Leverage customer testimonials and before-and-after photos to showcase the quality of your work. Collaborate with local businesses, such as garden centers or home improvement stores, to cross-promote services and reach a wider audience. Effective marketing and promotion will generate awareness and drive demand for your expanded service offerings.

Identifying additional services beyond lawn mowing is a strategic approach to growing your lawn care business. By conducting market research, leveraging your expertise and resources, diversifying service offerings, assessing profitability and demand, and implementing effective marketing strategies, you can successfully expand your service offerings and meet the evolving needs of your customers. Providing a comprehensive range of services will not only increase revenue but also establish your business as a one-stop solution for all lawn care needs, enhancing customer satisfaction and loyalty.

### Upselling and cross-selling opportunities.

Upselling and cross-selling are powerful strategies that can maximize revenue and enhance customer satisfaction in your lawn care business. By effectively identifying opportunities to upsell and cross-sell additional services or products, you can increase the value of each customer interaction and strengthen customer relationships. In this chapter, we will explore the importance of upselling and cross-selling, as well as strategies to capitalize on these opportunities in the context of a lawn care business. By implementing these strategies, you can drive business growth and provide added value to your customers.

Understand Customer Needs: To effectively upsell and cross-sell, it's crucial to understand your customers' needs and preferences. Take the time to listen to their concerns and goals for their outdoor spaces. Conduct a thorough assessment of their lawns, landscapes, and any existing services they may have. By gaining a comprehensive understanding of their needs, you can identify relevant upselling and cross-selling opportunities that provide value and address their specific requirements.

Upselling involves offering customers an upgraded or enhanced version of the service they initially requested. Consider the following strategies to identify upselling opportunities in your lawn care business:

> Enhanced Lawn Care Packages: Offer customers the option to upgrade their lawn care package to include additional services such as fertilization, weed control, or pest management. Highlight the benefits of these services, such as healthier and greener lawns or improved pest prevention.

Premium Products: Recommend premium products, such as high-quality grass seed, fertilizers, or landscaping materials, that can deliver better results and enhance the overall appearance of their outdoor spaces. Explain the advantages of these products and how they can contribute to a more vibrant and resilient lawn.

Seasonal Services: Inform customers about seasonal services that can enhance the health and aesthetics of their lawns. For example, recommend aeration and overseeding services in the fall to rejuvenate their turf or offer seasonal cleanup services to prepare their lawns for winter.

Cross-selling involves offering complementary services or products that align with the customer's needs. Consider the following strategies to identify cross-selling opportunities in your lawn care business:

When upselling or cross-selling, effective communication is key. Clearly explain the benefits and value of the additional services or products to the customer. Showcase how these offerings can address their specific needs and provide long-term benefits. Provide educational materials, such as brochures or online resources, that highlight the advantages of the upsell or cross-sell options. Take the time to answer any questions or concerns the customer may have, ensuring they feel confident in their decision.

Personalized Recommendations and Packages: Tailor your upselling and cross-selling recommendations to each customer's specific needs. Personalized recommendations demonstrate your attentiveness to their requirements and build trust. Consider creating bundled packages that combine complementary services or products at a discounted price, providing added value and incentive for customers to upgrade or add on services.

Upselling and cross-selling opportunities are valuable strategies for maximizing revenue and enhancing customer satisfaction in your lawn care business. By understanding customer needs, identifying upselling and cross-selling opportunities, effectively communicating the value of additional services or products, and providing personalized recommendations, you can successfully capitalize on these opportunities. By leveraging these strategies, you can not only increase your business's profitability but also enhance the overall customer experience, leading to long-term customer loyalty and business growth.

## Strategies for business growth and expansion

As a lawn care business owner, your goal is not only to maintain a successful operation but also to achieve sustainable growth and expansion. To achieve this, you need to implement effective strategies that will help you attract new customers, retain existing ones, and increase your revenue. In this chapter, we will explore various strategies for business growth and expansion in the context of a lawn care business. By leveraging these strategies, you can take your business to new heights and establish yourself as a leader in the industry.

One of the key strategies for business growth is to expand your service offerings beyond basic lawn care. Identify additional services that align with your business and cater to the needs of your target market. This can include services such as landscaping, tree and shrub care, irrigation system installation and maintenance, seasonal cleanups, or pest control. By diversifying your offerings, you can attract a wider range of customers and increase your revenue potential.

Consider expanding your reach by targeting new markets. This can involve focusing on specific geographical areas that are underserved by lawn care businesses or targeting niche markets with specialized needs, such as commercial properties, housing communities, or retirement communities. Conduct market research to identify potential opportunities and tailor your marketing efforts to effectively reach and attract customers in these new markets.

Collaborating with other businesses in related industries can be a powerful growth strategy. Seek out partnerships with garden centers, hardware stores, real estate agencies, or property management companies. These partnerships can lead to referrals, joint marketing efforts, and access to new customer bases. By leveraging the existing customer relationships and resources of your partners, you can expand your reach and drive business growth.

Invest in Marketing and Advertising. To attract new customers and increase your visibility, it's essential to invest in effective marketing and advertising strategies. Develop a strong online presence by creating a professional website, optimizing it for search engines, and utilizing social media platforms to engage with potential customers. Consider running targeted online advertising campaigns and leveraging local directories or community bulletin boards. Traditional advertising methods, such as print ads, direct mail, and local radio, can also be effective in reaching your target audience. Continuously track and analyze the performance of your marketing efforts to ensure maximum return on investment.

Focus on Customer Retention and Referrals: While attracting new customers is important, retaining existing ones and encouraging referrals are equally crucial for sustainable growth. Provide exceptional customer service, exceed expectations, and maintain consistent communication with your customers. Implement loyalty programs, referral incentives, or discounts for repeat business to encourage customer loyalty and word-of-mouth recommendations. Consider offering seasonal promotions or special offers to incentivize customers to book recurring services or refer your business to others.

Invest in Technology and Efficiency: Embrace technology to streamline your operations and improve efficiency. Invest in lawn care management software to automate scheduling, invoicing, and customer communication. Utilize GPS tracking systems to optimize routing and reduce travel time. Embrace digital tools for estimating, quoting, and project management. By adopting technology and streamlining processes, you can improve productivity, reduce costs, and deliver an exceptional customer experience.

Seek Opportunities for Expansion: Evaluate opportunities for expansion, such as acquiring existing lawn care businesses or franchising your business model. Acquiring established businesses can provide instant access to a customer base, infrastructure, and trained staff. Franchising allows you to replicate your successful business model in new markets with the support of franchisees. These expansion strategies require careful planning, financial analysis, and legal considerations, but they can offer significant opportunities for growth.

Implementing effective strategies for business growth and expansion is essential for long-term success in the lawn care industry. By expanding your service offerings, targeting new markets, developing strategic partnerships, investing in marketing and advertising, focusing on customer retention and referrals, embracing technology and efficiency, and seeking opportunities for expansion, you can position your business for sustainable growth. Continuously monitor and adapt your strategies based on market trends, customer feedback, and industry developments to stay ahead of the competition and achieve your growth objectives.

## Chapter 10: Overcoming Challenges and Ensuring Long-Term Success

**Common challenges in the lawn mowing business and how to overcome them.**

Running a lawn care business can be a rewarding venture, but it also comes with its fair share of challenges. From fierce competition and changing market dynamics to managing customer expectations and keeping up with industry trends, it's important to proactively address these obstacles to ensure the long-term success and sustainability of your business. In this chapter, we will explore the key challenges faced by lawn care business owners and provide practical strategies for overcoming them. By adopting a proactive and solution-oriented mindset, you can navigate through these challenges and position your business for long-term success.

Seasonality and Weather Conditions:

The lawn mowing business is highly seasonal, with demand peaking during the spring and summer months. Additionally, adverse weather conditions such as rain or drought can impact scheduling and revenue.

To overcome seasonality challenges, consider diversifying your service offerings beyond lawn mowing. Offer services like landscaping, fertilization, or snow removal during the offseason to generate additional revenue. Develop a marketing plan to promote these services to your existing customer base and target new customers in need of year-round maintenance. During unpredictable weather, maintain open communication with customers, reschedule appointments when necessary, and provide alternative services, such as cleanup or maintenance tasks, on rainy or hot days.

Intense Competition:

The lawn care industry is highly competitive, with numerous companies vying for the same customers. Standing out and attracting new clients can be challenging.

Focus on differentiating your business from competitors. Highlight your unique selling points, such as exceptional customer service, attention to detail, or specialized expertise. Emphasize these qualities in your marketing materials and communicate them effectively to potential customers. Leverage customer testimonials and online reviews to showcase your reputation and build trust. Offer competitive pricing, bundle services, or provide added value to attract new clients. Additionally, invest in professional branding and a user-friendly website to create a strong online presence and improve your visibility.

Hiring and Retaining Skilled Staff:

Finding and retaining reliable, skilled workers can be a significant challenge in the lawn mowing industry. High turnover rates and labor shortages can disrupt operations and impact customer satisfaction.

Develop a comprehensive recruitment strategy to attract quality candidates. Advertise job openings through online job boards, social media, and local community networks. Screen applicants thoroughly, conduct interviews, and check references to ensure a good fit. Offer competitive wages and benefits to attract and retain talented employees. Provide ongoing training and opportunities for professional development to enhance their skills and job satisfaction. Cultivate a positive work environment that fosters teamwork, communication, and recognition. By investing in your employees, you can build a loyal and motivated team that contributes to the success of your business.

Customer Service and Satisfaction:
Meeting customer expectations and ensuring satisfaction can be challenging, as preferences and requirements can vary from one customer to another.

Prioritize clear and open communication with customers. Take the time to understand their specific needs and preferences. Provide detailed service agreements or contracts to manage expectations. Regularly communicate with customers to address any concerns or questions they may have. Train your employees to deliver excellent customer service, emphasizing professionalism, reliability, and attentiveness. Actively seek customer feedback and use it to improve your service offerings. Go above and beyond to exceed customer expectations whenever possible.

Equipment Maintenance and Repair:
Maintaining and repairing lawn mowing equipment can be a time-consuming and costly task. Equipment breakdowns can disrupt operations and impact customer satisfaction.

Implement a regular maintenance schedule for your equipment. Follow manufacturer guidelines for maintenance and conduct routine inspections to identify any issues early on. Keep spare parts on hand and establish relationships with local equipment suppliers or repair services for quick assistance when needed. Consider investing in high-quality equipment that is known for its durability and reliability. Train your employees on proper equipment use and maintenance to prevent avoidable breakdowns. By prioritizing equipment care and maintenance, you can minimize disruptions and ensure efficient operations.

Running a lawn mowing business may present challenges, but with the right strategies, these obstacles can be overcome. By diversifying your services, differentiating from competitors, hiring and retaining skilled staff, providing excellent customer service, and maintaining equipment effectively, you can navigate through common challenges and achieve long-term success in the lawn care industry. Adaptability, continuous improvement, and a customer-centric approach are key to overcoming these challenges and thriving in a competitive market.

### Staying competitive in a dynamic market.

In today's dynamic market, it's crucial for your lawn care business to stay competitive and adapt to changing trends and customer demands. By implementing the following strategies, you can position your business for success and stand out from the competition:

Stay Current with Industry Trends. Keep a pulse on the latest industry trends, technological advancements, and best practices in the lawn care business. Subscribe to industry publications, attend trade shows and conferences, and participate in professional networks to stay informed. By staying current, you can identify emerging opportunities, incorporate innovative techniques and technologies, and offer cutting-edge services to your customers.

Offer Specialized Services. Differentiate your business by offering specialized services that cater to specific customer needs. Consider expanding your service offerings beyond traditional lawn mowing to include landscaping, irrigation installation and maintenance, pest control, or organic lawn care. By providing a comprehensive range of services, you can become a one-stop solution for your customers and capture a larger market share.

Embrace Sustainable Practices. With an increasing focus on environmental sustainability, adopting eco-friendly practices can give your business a competitive edge. Use organic fertilizers, promote water conservation measures, and offer alternative lawn care options that minimize the use of chemicals. Highlight your commitment to sustainability in your marketing efforts to attract environmentally-conscious customers who value eco-friendly services.

Invest in Technology. Leverage technology to streamline your operations, enhance customer experience, and improve efficiency. Utilize lawn care management software for scheduling, invoicing, and customer management. Implement GPS tracking systems to optimize route planning and reduce travel time. Embrace online platforms and mobile apps for easy customer communication and appointment bookings. By embracing technology, you can automate processes, improve productivity, and provide a seamless experience for your customers.

Focus on Customer Experience. Providing exceptional customer service and a positive experience is key to standing out in a competitive market. Prioritize communication by promptly responding to customer inquiries, providing transparent pricing, and keeping customers informed about their service schedules. Personalize your interactions with customers and show genuine care for their needs and concerns. Encourage customer feedback and use it to improve your services. Happy customers are more likely to become loyal advocates and refer your business to others.

Build Strong Online Presence. In today's digital age, having a strong online presence is essential for attracting customers. Develop a professional website that showcases your services, testimonials, and contact information. Optimize your website for search engines to improve your visibility. Leverage social media platforms to engage with your target audience, share relevant content, and run targeted advertising campaigns. Encourage satisfied customers to leave reviews and ratings on online platforms. A strong online presence helps build credibility, reach a wider audience, and generate leads.

Competitive pricing is crucial in a dynamic market. Conduct market research to understand the pricing landscape and determine competitive rates for your services. Consider factors such as your costs, value-added services, and the local market demand. Offer transparent pricing and clearly communicate the value customers will receive from your services. Additionally, periodically evaluate your pricing strategy to ensure it remains competitive and profitable.

In conclusion, staying competitive in a dynamic market requires a combination of adaptability, innovation, and a customer-centric approach. By staying informed, offering specialized services, embracing sustainability, leveraging technology, prioritizing customer experience, building an online presence, and maintaining competitive pricing, you can differentiate your lawn care business and thrive in a competitive landscape. Continuously assess market trends, customer preferences, and industry developments to stay ahead and continuously improve your offerings.

### Planning for the future and adapting to industry changes

In the ever-evolving lawn care industry, planning for the future and adapting to industry changes are vital for the long-term success of your business. By proactively preparing for the future and staying ahead of industry trends, you can position your lawn care business for growth and navigate through challenges. Here are some strategies to help you plan for the future and adapt to industry changes:

Conduct market research and Analysis to stay informed about the current market trends, customer preferences, and emerging opportunities in the lawn care industry. Conduct market research and analysis to identify shifts in customer needs, changes in demographics, and emerging technologies. Keep a close eye on your competitors and industry leaders to understand their strategies and innovations. By understanding the market landscape, you can make informed decisions and adjust your business approach accordingly.

A comprehensive business plan serves as a roadmap for the future of your lawn care business. Define your long-term goals, objectives, and strategies. Identify areas of growth, potential challenges, and opportunities for diversification. Outline your marketing and sales strategies, operational plans, and financial projections. Regularly review and update your business plan to reflect changes in the industry and align with your evolving goals. A solid business plan provides clarity and direction, enabling you to adapt to industry changes and make informed decisions.

Technology plays a crucial role in the lawn care industry, and embracing it can give your business a competitive edge. Stay updated on the latest technological advancements in the field, such as automated irrigation systems, remote monitoring tools, or drone technology for aerial surveys. Evaluate which technologies can enhance your operations, improve efficiency, and deliver better customer experiences. Invest in software solutions for scheduling, invoicing, and customer relationship management. By leveraging technology, you can streamline processes, increase productivity, and stay ahead of industry changes.

Foster a culture of innovation! Encourage a culture of innovation within your organization. Create an environment where employees feel empowered to suggest ideas and solutions for improving operations and delivering better services. Regularly assess your service offerings and explore opportunities to introduce new services or improve existing ones. Stay open to feedback from your customers and employees and use it as a source of inspiration for innovation. By fostering a culture of innovation, you can adapt to industry changes, meet evolving customer demands, and differentiate your business.

As an industry professional, it is essential to invest in your own professional development and that of your team. Stay updated on industry best practices, certifications, and training opportunities. Attend industry conferences, workshops, and webinars to expand your knowledge and network with fellow professionals. Encourage your employees to participate in training programs and provide them with opportunities for growth and skill development. By continually learning and evolving, you can stay competitive, offer high-quality services, and adapt to changing industry standards.

Diversification can help you expand your customer base, mitigate risks, and adapt to industry changes. Assess the needs of your target market and identify additional services that complement your existing lawn care offerings. Consider incorporating services such as landscaping, hardscaping, tree care, or pest control. By offering a comprehensive range of services, you can cater to a wider range of customer needs and create additional revenue streams.

Regularly seek feedback from your customers to gauge their satisfaction and identify areas for improvement. Implement customer satisfaction surveys, encourage online reviews, and maintain open lines of communication. Analyze the feedback received and take proactive steps to address any concerns or suggestions. By actively listening to your customers and responding to their needs, you can build strong customer relationships, enhance loyalty, and adapt your services to meet their evolving expectations.

The lawn care industry is subject to various regulations, such as licensing, permits, and environmental guidelines. Stay informed about the regulatory requirements in your area and ensure your business operates in compliance with all applicable laws. Regularly review and update your business practices to align with changing regulations. By staying compliant, you can protect your business from legal issues, maintain a positive reputation, and position yourself as a trustworthy and responsible service provider.

Planning for the future and adapting to industry changes are essential for the long-term success of your lawn care business. By conducting market research, developing a strategic business plan, embracing technology and innovation, fostering a culture of innovation, investing in professional development, diversifying service offerings, monitoring customer feedback, and staying compliant with regulations, you can position your business for growth and effectively navigate through industry changes. Remember, adaptability and agility are key to thriving in a dynamic market, so stay proactive and embrace opportunities for growth and improvement.

## Key Lessons and Takeaways

Running a lawn care business can be a rewarding venture, but it also comes with its fair share of challenges. From fierce competition and changing market dynamics to managing customer expectations and keeping up with industry trends, it's important to proactively address these obstacles to ensure the long-term success and sustainability of your business. In this chapter, we will explore the key challenges faced by lawn care business owners and provide practical strategies for overcoming them. By adopting a proactive and solution-oriented mindset, you can navigate through these challenges and position your business for long-term success.

Adapting to Market Dynamics:

The lawn care industry is subject to various market dynamics, such as seasonality, weather conditions, and economic fluctuations. To overcome these challenges, it's essential to develop a solid understanding of market trends and adapt your business strategies accordingly. Implement seasonal marketing campaigns, diversify your service offerings to cater to different customer needs throughout the year, and consider expanding into complementary areas, such as landscaping or snow removal during the offseason. By staying agile and responsive to market changes, you can mitigate the impact of seasonality and maintain a steady stream of revenue.

Differentiating from Competitors:

Competition in the lawn care industry can be intense, making it crucial to differentiate your business from others. Identify your unique selling points and emphasize them in your marketing efforts. Whether it's your exceptional customer service, specialized expertise, eco-friendly practices, or innovative technology, highlight what sets your business apart. Foster strong relationships with your customers by providing personalized attention, going the extra mile, and consistently delivering high-quality results. By differentiating your business, you can attract and retain loyal customers who appreciate the value you provide.

Managing Customer Expectations:

Customer satisfaction is paramount in the lawn care industry, and managing customer expectations can be challenging. Clear communication, setting realistic expectations, and delivering on promises are key to ensuring customer satisfaction. Take the time to understand your customers' needs and preferences, provide detailed service agreements or contracts, and communicate any limitations or potential challenges upfront. Regularly communicate with your customers, address their concerns promptly, and consistently strive to exceed their expectations. By prioritizing customer satisfaction, you can build strong relationships, earn positive reviews and referrals, and secure long-term success.

Optimizing Operations and Efficiency:

Efficient operations are essential for long-term success in the lawn care business. Streamline your processes by leveraging technology and automation. Invest in lawn care management software to simplify scheduling, routing, and invoicing. Utilize GPS tracking systems to optimize travel routes and reduce fuel costs. Regularly assess your workflows to identify areas for improvement and implement efficient systems to maximize productivity. By optimizing operations, you can save time, reduce costs, and provide a more streamlined and professional experience for your customers.

Building a Skilled and Motivated Team:

Your team plays a crucial role in the success of your lawn care business. Hiring and retaining skilled and motivated employees is essential. Develop a strong recruitment strategy to attract qualified candidates, conduct thorough interviews, and check references. Provide ongoing training and development opportunities to enhance their skills and knowledge. Foster a positive work culture that values teamwork, collaboration, and open communication. Recognize and reward employee achievements to boost morale and maintain motivation. By investing in your team, you can build a competent and dedicated workforce that contributes to the long-term success of your business.

Staying Informed and Continuously Learning:

The lawn care industry is constantly evolving, with new techniques, technologies, and regulations emerging. Staying informed and continuously learning is crucial to adapt and thrive. Attend industry conferences, workshops, and trade shows to stay updated on the latest trends and best practices. Join professional associations and networks to connect with peers and learn from their experiences. Subscribe to industry publications and online forums to access valuable insights and resources. By prioritizing continuous learning, you can stay ahead of the curve, offer innovative solutions to your customers, and position your business for long-term success.

Congratulations on completing "The Ultimate Guide to Starting a Successful Lawn Mowing Business." Armed with the knowledge and insights gained throughout this journey, you are well-equipped to embark on your entrepreneurial adventure in the lawn care industry. As you set out to turn your dreams into reality, here are some final words of encouragement and motivation to fuel your success: Embrace Your Passion:

Remember the passion that sparked your desire to start a lawn mowing business. Let that passion guide you through the ups and downs of entrepreneurship. It will be your driving force, motivating you to provide exceptional service and exceed customer expectations. Your enthusiasm will resonate with your clients and set you apart from the competition.

Embrace Continuous Learning:

The journey of entrepreneurship is an ongoing learning experience. Stay curious, embrace new ideas, and adapt to industry changes. Seek opportunities to expand your knowledge, network with industry professionals, and stay updated on the latest trends and technologies. Never stop learning and growing, as it will keep your business relevant and thriving.

Embrace Resilience:

Entrepreneurship comes with its fair share of challenges and setbacks. The key is to embrace resilience and develop the ability to bounce back from adversity. Stay committed to your vision, remain adaptable, and view obstacles as opportunities for growth. Remember that every setback is a chance to learn, refine your strategies, and come back stronger than before.

Embrace the Power of Relationships:

Building strong relationships with your customers, employees, and industry peers is crucial for long-term success. Prioritize excellent customer service, foster a positive work culture, and seek collaborations within the industry. These relationships will not only enhance your business but also provide support and guidance during challenging times.

Embrace Innovation:

The lawn care industry is evolving, and embracing innovation is key to staying ahead. Embrace new technologies, explore new service offerings, and constantly seek ways to improve efficiency and customer experiences. By staying at the forefront of innovation, you can position your business as a leader in the industry.

Embrace Adaptability:

The business landscape is ever-changing, and adaptability is a fundamental skill for success. Stay flexible, monitor market conditions, and be willing to adapt your strategies and services to meet evolving customer needs. By staying adaptable, you can navigate industry changes, capitalize on emerging opportunities, and remain competitive.

Embrace Your Vision:

As you embark on your entrepreneurial journey, hold onto your vision and let it guide your decisions. Stay focused on your long-term goals, but also be open to adjusting your path as you gain new insights and experiences. Stay true to your values, maintain a strong work ethic, and never lose sight of the impact you want to make with your business.

Remember, starting a successful lawn mowing business requires dedication, hard work, and a commitment to excellence. Believe in yourself, trust the process, and embrace the opportunities and challenges that come your way. With passion, perseverance, and the knowledge you have gained, you are well on your way to building a thriving and prosperous lawn care business. Best of luck on your entrepreneurial journey!

www.ingramcontent.com/pod-product-compliance
Lightning Source LLC
Chambersburg PA
CBHW070115230526
45472CB00004B/1266